Conscious Revolution

THE AWAKENING OF SOULS

MAVEN PRESS

Copyright © Laura Elizabeth
First published in Australia in 2022
by Maven Press
Roleystone WA 6111

Edited by Jade Bell

All rights reserved. No part of this book may be used or reproduced by any means, graphic, electronic, or mechanical, including photocopying, recording, taping or by any information storage retrieval system without the written permission of the copyright owner except in the case of brief quotations embodied in critical articles and reviews.

Because of the dynamic nature of the Internet, any web addresses or links contained in this book may have changed since publication and may no longer be vaild. The views expressed in this work are solely those of the author and do not necessarily reflect the views of the publisher and the publisher hereby disclaims any responsibility for them.

 A catalogue record for this work is available from the National Library of Australia

National Library of Australia Catalogue-in-Publication data:
Conscious Revolution/Laura Elizabeth

ISBN: 978-0-6456356-3-8
(Paperback)

ISBN: 978-0-6456356-4-5
(Ebook)

To those courageous enough to know better and do better, creating the life they desire from a place of love.

Foreword

DR. RICCI-JANE ADAMS

As I began to write the foreword for *Conscious Revolution,* I was very focused on the first word—conscious. I asked lots of questions about what it meant to the authors. Is conscious used in the same way as consciousness? What does the title of this book want me to understand about being conscious? But something happened as I read the words of each incredible author and steeped myself in their extraordinary stories.

The word that really matters in the title of this book is *revolutionary.* For that is what each of these women is—a revolutionary.

Each woman's story is gobsmacking. These women not only survived the trauma of their lives, but also chose to awaken through these events. Beyond that, they have decided to serve through the wisdom of their lived experience.

The great contemporary mystic, Caroline Myss, asks a question I have asked myself many times. *What will you do with your pain?*

The larger quote from *Anatomy of the Spirit* states, 'We will all have experiences meant to "break our hearts" – not in half but wide open. Regardless of how your heart is broken, your choice is always the same: What will you do with your pain?'

The women in this book have all chosen to show up in service to the greater good despite their pain. Perhaps more accurately, they have made a conscious effort to see the deeper meaning of their pain and not let the events of their lives limit them, box them in or slow them down. This is profoundly revolutionary.

I have spent a lot of time considering what it is to be revolutionary.

When I began the Institute for Intuitive Intelligence, I knew I wanted to do things differently in the space of intuition education. I quickly understood that when a woman stands up and questions the status quo, she is often immediately considered difficult and disavowed.

In trying to bring a deeper understanding of intuition to the contemporary spiritual world, something that seemed obvious and reasonable to me, I was considered difficult. I noticed people strongly reacted to me—they either loved or hated me, nothing in between. To my mind, I was simply trying to do things better. In breaking the mold, I was disrupting the status quo and making people feel uncomfortable.

I am sure every woman in this book has been accused of being difficult and noncompliant. I hope she wears it as a badge of honor. In choosing to raise her consciousness and do things better, a woman becomes a disruptor. This will not be welcomed. In fact, it will often be outright rejected. But here is something I have come to understand on my own conscious revolution: I was not placed on this earth for my comfort nor yours. I was placed here for my evolution (and yours).

In a materialistic world, terrified of change, to privilege the spiritual and evolutionary is to be considered revolutionary. When I asked the divine Laura Elizabeth, creator of Maven Press, to define the title and intention of this book, she said, 'It's like the moment that your consciousness remembers it is conscious.' This book is a collection of the moments when these extraordinary women became conscious of their consciousness or went deeper into their own conscious awakening.

I love a resilient woman, but one who has awakened to her spiritual nature. Well, she is my kind of woman. To privilege the spiritual and the holy, even when life has caused pain and suffering is the ultimate flex. These women are congruent. They walk their talk. With humility, grace, and power, they share the moments in which their consciousness became conscious in order to allow us to awaken to ourselves.

When women decide to get conscious of their lives, the whole world changes. I honestly believe that for many women who choose to live outside of the box, this simple choice alone feels revolutionary.

I adore reading the many references to intuition scattered throughout this book. Without a doubt, that conscious revolution is so often brought about by deep intuitive knowing. The courage to follow that intuition is what allows for more consciousness to rise and awaken, not only in ourselves but in the world.

Intuition is my jam. In my definition, it is the language of consciousness. To live in and through our intuition is what it is to become conscious. To follow that intuition where it leads, even when we don't know the destination, is what makes it revolutionary.

I am lucky enough to know three of the authors in this exceptional book personally. After reading each chapter, I feel I know all of these authors intimately. Each author writes with such generosity and transparency. Along with deeply profound stories of conscious revolution, there are practical tools, processes, tips, and deep wisdom designed to save us from the struggle and pain these great teachers have survived. I strongly recommend reading this book with a pen in hand or a journal by your side. Take detailed notes. Listen hard. Lean in.

These stories, individually, are profound and humbling. Each author's contribution takes on greater significance when woven together in the rich tapestry that is *Conscious Revolution*. Despite living in a world that was not made for the awakened woman, nevertheless, she persisted. The threads of one event, one story, and one deep wisdom are found in the next and the next. To read this book as a whole is to meet the ultimate girl gang. Goddess gang, more accurately!

Conscious Revolution is a rich tapestry populated by badass conscious revolutionaries. Every word has inspired me, and I bow to each author's humility, grace, and power. In reading this book, let yourself be inspired to know that this is you, too. All that these women have done with adversity to awaken their souls is possible for us all. Thank you for showing us the way, dear revolutionary.

About Dr. Ricci-Jane

My name is Dr. Ricci-Jane Adams, and I am the principal of the Institute for Intuitive Intelligence, a world-class, global professional intuition training school. I am a mentor and teacher for the spiritually fierce and the author of the bestselling *Spiritually Fierce, Intuitive Intelligence Training,* and *Superconscious Intuition*. I have a doctorate from the University of Melbourne in magical realism. I have spent over twenty-five years devoted to spiritual awakening and am a qualified transpersonal counsellor.

Find me at:
Website: *instituteforintuitiveintelligence.com*
Instagram: *instagram.com/intuitiveintelligenceinstitute*

Contents

Sonja Harvey
DISCOVERING YOURSELF 1

Krista Hammerbacher Haapala
ALIGN AND FLOW WITH YOUR PLEASURE REVOLUTION 14

Enisa Cuturich
MY JOURNEY TO UNLEASH ENISA 23

Nila Matthews
AWAKENING FLOW WITH CONSCIOUS CREATIVITY 38

Ash Moreland
WHO AM I? 58

Samantha-Jayne Love
MY CUP IS FULL 73

Mitzi Rae
CHILDREN AT HEART 86

Jenny Arnold
I KNOW WHICH WAY I'M GOING 104

Conny Wladkowski
SPIRITUAL AWAKENING 114

Jade Bell
A WAY FORWARD 125

Laura Elizabeth
THE CHOICE IS YOURS 135

Sonja Harvey

DISCOVERING YOURSELF

For as long as I can remember, I've been a seeker. I've always been deeply curious, driving my poor mom crazy growing up with my incessant 'But why?' questions. I love learning, and my curiosity has mostly served me well. It's my nature to want to understand and get beyond the surface of things, to uncover the roots obscured from view. It helps me organize and make sense of the world, especially when very little seems to at times. The downside is that it can keep me in my conscious reasoning mind, blocking access to my intuition and deepest knowing.

One of the more profound takeaways from my journey is understanding that fear is an invitation *and* a bridge. If we look more closely at what scares us and why and meet it with curiosity, we can experience our fear as an invitation to bring something into our conscious awareness. Something that's been trying to get our attention. Doing the work to clear out subconscious fear is the bridge. It spans the distance between what keeps us small, contracted, and driven by what lies below our conscious awareness. The bridge takes us to where we can meet all of who we are, and we can start trusting in our intuition and expanding our capacity to live and lead more consciously.

It's the path I see in retrospect that became a parallel journey for me. This innate desire of mine to learn and raise my conscious awareness coincided with my career progression in leadership. It's the culmination of my lived experience and why I lead the way I do today. Looking back on my younger self, however, there are so many things I wish I had known when I started my career.

For one, I would sit my younger self down and share that no one really knows what they're doing. But we're all trying to figure it out as we go, especially as leaders.

I would gently tell my younger, naïve self that her need to be right was just her ego getting in the way, not the pathway to demonstrating her value. It was, however, a surefire way to piss people off.

I would encourage her to follow her inner voice, clarifying that *was* the way forward. She'll eventually realize this is her intuition, and she can trust it. Not push it aside repeatedly, listening instead to what someone else believed was best for her. We alone are the authority of our life and our life choices.

I would've told her to trust her instincts and feelings, even if she didn't have the words to articulate their meaning yet. But when she did, to use her voice and tell her truth, let go of her need to please everyone but herself.

I would have comforted her when she felt frozen by her fear, unable to do anything but remain silent. When she said 'yes' but really meant 'no'. When the risk of disappointing others outweighed what she knew was best for her, causing her to doubt herself time and again.

So small and fragile was her belief in herself. I wish I could've held up a mirror to show her all of who she was. I wonder at times where my life would've taken me if I had believed in myself sooner. Saw my fear as the invitation and the bridge. Trusted my intuition earlier. Looked for what I needed from within instead of from outside of me.

I will never know the answer to these questions, but I trust that my life unfolded exactly as it needed to for me to learn each of these lessons in my divine timing. My desire to better understand myself and others, coupled with my conscious revolution, facilitated my personal development and my growth as a leader. I hope that by sharing some of my story, you'll be able to answer and embody these questions in your life much earlier than I did.

~

My career has been the biggest vehicle for my personal growth and has seen some significant and extreme pendulum swings. In my earliest leadership role, I came in guns blazing, eager to prove myself. My headstrong, solution-oriented approach and my fear of being seen as inexperienced outweighed the awareness that there were unspoken but very real social norms and nuances to which I should have been conforming. I was shocked more than a few times by my colleague's reactions to what, to me, seemed the obvious questions to be asking. My innocent but very public questioning of operational decisions was not appreciated nor welcome. Here I was trying to prove my value as the new and youngest leader at the table. I was shedding light on problems I believed needed discussing, and with some urgency, only to realize too late that these were things we didn't question, let alone talk about openly. I clearly missed that memo in my orientation package.

It was incredibly frustrating. None of it made any logical sense to me. It took me a minute (read years) to recognize that questioning their authority would put me, not them, in a difficult position. I was the outlier, the exception. I had not conformed to the organizational culture and got hammered for it. My behavior threatened the status quo, which, in this case, was a culture of complacency. My refusal to leave the matter alone only served to widen the gap between us. As you can imagine, I was not very popular in those early days. Case in point: a few long-time employees banded together to have me fired. They were not successful, but the fact remained that I made people uncomfortable, and to make matters worse, I was oblivious to that fact.

While I did a lot of reflective, analytical thinking, I was not exactly self-aware in these early career days. I was stuck in my head, trying to think my way out of things, desperately hoping to prove I was right and worthy of being at the leadership table. I didn't realize how self-absorbed and self-righteous I was. I needed to talk less, listen more, and try to relate to where they were coming from. To have some empathy and appreciate how it must have felt for them not to know how to deal with these organizational challenges, fearing what those changes would mean for their *own* sense of comfort and job security. I had no conscious awareness of these needs and certainly no compassion, so I made many mistakes.

It was a deeply humbling learning experience and a turning point for me. I changed my university major in my final year to pursue a degree in psychology, becoming a card-carrying, lifelong student of human nature. I had so much to learn and was impatient to learn it all. I was drawn to everything and everyone who could shed new light on why we (read me) behave the way we do. I met a teacher and business mentor during this time who seemed to have it all figured out.

His abundance of confidence and ability to make sense of what still felt nonsensical to me drew me in. He was charismatic, off-the-charts intelligent, and he made me feel fully seen and heard in a way I never had before. It was intoxicating. Whatever this guy had, I wanted it, and I became a sponge for all he could teach me. He was also all about results, and after working in an organization where very little changed over time, I was all in. I also began to silence my voice, allowing the pendulum to swing to the other extreme. I slowly replaced my voice with someone else's who I deemed more intelligent, better informed, and more worthy.

Over time, as I unconsciously let go of more and more of myself, making room for his larger-than-life persona, his behavior became more controlling. The shift was subtle at first, until it wasn't. His voice became the one in my head, directing my next move, often my next thought. Even then, I wasn't doing it right. I always seemed to miss something critical, causing him to become frustrated and angry, often volatile. By this point, we had transitioned from a coaching relationship into a business partnership, and I was both emotionally and financially entangled with him.

I lived in some degree of fear every single day of this four-year partnership. I dreaded going to work because I knew I would do, say, or not do something that would set him off at some point. I withdrew from my friends and family, not knowing how to talk about what I was experiencing and feeling deeply ashamed that I wasn't measuring up. I declined just about everything that took my focus off work. On a rare occasion, I remember being at a dear friend's wedding, looking at my watch repeatedly, trying to figure out when I could sneak out. I was anxious that he would call to check in, learning I wasn't at home diligently working that Saturday evening.

My fear was an invitation to look more closely at this dynamic. To sit with my deepest truth and my inner knowing that I needed to get out. But I did not explore it. I didn't have the capacity at that time. Instead, I used it as a weapon against myself. My fear, unchecked, became the reinforcement that I was not intelligent, worthy, or insightful enough, that I wasn't trying hard enough. I was a disappointment and a waste of his time. My nervous system was frozen in this time and place. I did not trust myself. I couldn't even *hear* myself any longer.

I was separated from my support systems, and I was also going through a divorce. I was vulnerable when this partnership began and initially felt relieved that someone else wanted to show me the way forward. He was opportunistic, patient, and manipulative in his grooming of me, including his reassurances that I could leave at any time. That staying was my choice and mine alone. What made it infinitely more confusing for me was that I *was* learning from him despite all this turmoil.

I have so much compassion for this young woman as I reflect on her. Her ego was drawn in by the promise of what she could learn and who she could become professionally. She worked hard to meet ever-evolving expectations that were impossible to reach. She took responsibility for what she believed were her many failures, buying into the toxic and destructive messaging she heard on repeat, taking solace in the rare occasions he offered a crumb of praise until she was unable to any longer.

At some point, I just stopped. I pretended to go through the motions, but there was no energy or feeling behind them. I could not find the strength or the words to stand up to him. I only found my way out when he realized there was no longer work taking place. He could not rely on me, so he kicked me out.

I've asked myself hundreds of times what you are likely thinking now. How could I not walk away from this on my own? Why did I stay for so long? Why was I working so hard to gain his approval despite his abusive behavior?

Because I believed him, I abandoned myself. I pushed my voice aside so frequently that I stopped even noticing it. My psychology degree was no match for this trauma. I couldn't think my way out of this one. I was numb to feeling anything by this point, and I was completely cut off from my intuition.

Once I was out, the relief and the panic came in equal waves. I was grateful to be free, but my business was in shambles, I was in financial ruin, and I had no idea what I would do. But I could hear myself again, faintly, and that was enough.

It took me several years to find my footing again. I coasted in a few jobs that gave me a safe place to land and a consistent paycheck while I sorted through the wreckage that was my life. I let go of the ambition I once embraced so fiercely and allowed myself time and space to heal.

Almost without my noticing it, I started saying yes to leadership opportunities. I found myself taking on roles I wasn't exactly ready for but knew I could figure out. The fear that would have previously held me back was replaced with a feeling that *maybe I could do it*, along with a desire to try. It was as if my system was defrosting, and I could finally feel again. As I unpacked the fear around my initial hesitations at these opportunities, I realized there was likely nothing that would be as bad as what I had come through. The full appreciation that I *had* come through it, that I was on the other side, became a gift.

As my self-awareness increased, so did my trust in *self*. I became skilled at listening to what was being said and what wasn't. I began to trust what I was feeling, what I would now name my intuition, and was able to read the room much better. I could pick up on the undercurrents, the sticking points, and the areas where we didn't have an agreement or full support for an initiative. That allowed me to ask better questions and go about discussing the elephant in the room without making anyone feel confronted or to blame. I also, not surprisingly, became incredibly sensitive to rooting out toxic and incongruent leadership.

My commitment to my *own* conscious awareness and personal growth unquestionably made me a more effective leader. My earlier experiences taught me how important it was to create safety and take the time to build genuine rapport with my team. Wanting to be the leader I wish I had, I shared more of my own experiences and vulnerabilities first, hoping it would allow others to feel comfortable enough to voice their own. It gave us a place to build from and come together as a team. And it worked.

My team and my clients trusted me, and we were able to make some incredible things happen together. It is some of the most rewarding work I've been part of to date; so gratifying to demonstrate how we can transform organizational culture and drive results as we get behind a common goal and work together.

I was acutely aware that I never wanted anyone on my team to feel anything close to how I had in my partnership, nor did I want to make the same unconscious mistakes I had in my earliest leadership role. But I overcompensated and leaned into an unhealthy pattern that had me consistently putting the needs of others, their comfort, well above my own.

AS THE PENDULUM SWINGS

Here I am again, ignoring my intuition which screamed at me to slow down for more months than I care to admit. I was deeply grateful for this chapter in my career, working with such an amazing team and seeing our work's impact in the sector. After seven years, however, I was bone tired and wanted more from my life than just work. At this stage, I allowed my need to please others by remaining loyal to the organization, team, and client base to matter more than what I knew was true for me. I had abandoned myself again, albeit in a different way.

As a result, I crashed and burned hard. Medically, I had several issues that crept up on me and one that I couldn't ignore, although I did try. A few days before the Christmas holiday break, I was sitting in a team meeting when I started to feel a strange, uncomfortable pain in my jaw. It moved into my neck, then down my arm, and stayed there like a vice grip. I knew something was wrong. As I broke out into a cold sweat and tried to breathe through the discomfort, the thought crept into my mind that I might be having a heart attack. But what did I do? I said nothing and finished the remaining forty-five minutes of that meeting. Yup, I did!

So entrenched in the go, go, go grind, especially just before the holidays, I stayed quiet, deciding not to cause discomfort to anyone else. Given my stubbornness, it took me a while to get properly checked out after this event. I was in some deep denial. Thankfully, there was no permanent damage to my heart, but I missed the window that could've confirmed one way or another whether I'd had a mild heart attack or not. What I did have was a massive wake-up call that it was time to re-evaluate my choices again.

It's still hard for me to look at the example I was setting as a leader in this organization. I had been unintentionally and unconsciously perpetuating a narrow, unhealthy, and unrealistic model of leadership. I was portraying the exact opposite behavior I wanted to encourage in others. The resistance I had to slow down and listen to my intuition reinforced the unsustainable tone and pace I was setting. I was actively distracting myself from the truth that I was no longer happy there and had no idea what I wanted to do instead. Hello, fear, my old friend.

~

I have spent much of my professional life swinging from one extreme to another like a pendulum. Those extremes were created by reacting unconsciously to the events in my life and the aspects of myself I didn't want to face, having deemed them unworthy, unwelcome, and undesirable. Never slowing down or reflecting deeply enough to uncover what I was actually running from. Not realizing that avoiding my fear would ensure it would continue to influence my life and drive my behavior.

That pendulum also swung through the center each time. I just wasn't consciously aware enough to notice. I didn't give myself that time and space, and I wasn't skilled enough to attune to and trust my intuition. To learn how to live from a more balanced, conscious center point. By learning to meet our fear, we can clear the noise that keeps our intuition hidden from us.

How do we know the difference between our intuition and our fear? First, remember that fear is the ego's way of keeping us small and contracted, firmly planted in our comfort zone, which often doesn't feel comfortable. Its goal is to keep us safe, but it often keeps us imprisoned. Your intuition is calling you to something deeper, which may still scare you, but with some discernment, you learn to trust that calling, knowing it's for both your own and others' greatest good.

So, let's clear the noise and speed up this process, shall we?

Start by creating space for yourself just to sit still. Truth be told, this was the hardest part for me in the beginning. I was used to perpetual motion, and stillness felt foreign and very uncomfortable. Lean *into* that. It's completely normal; all you need to do is notice it. No judgment. No action steps. Just sit with it.

Create the space. Close the door. Let your household know you need some time without being disturbed. Start with three minutes. Don't feel you need to jump into an hour of stillness or meditation to prove you can. Start where you are with a few minutes of stillness, noticing your breath.

Can you be curious about whatever may be surfacing? As feelings or sensations arise, can you look at them like an outside observer might? Are you feeling it somewhere in your body? When a feeling or sensation is clear and present for you, can you ask it if there's anything deeper than that?

Maybe your three minutes of stillness evolve into fifteen one day. You may even begin to crave that feeling of stillness, that exquisite quiet, each day. That's what has unfolded for me. This devotional time is now a non-negotiable start of every day for me. It's where I can hear myself most clearly. Where I can unpack my fear and uncover what my soul wants me to know. It creates that critical space for me between the feeling and the doing that allows me to respond, to the best of my ability, consciously and purposefully. It doesn't mean I show up perfectly. It means I am actively working towards aligning my behavior with my values, that I am humble enough to acknowledge when I've not succeeded, and the first to go back to work to learn from it. It's been a game changer for me with respect to how I show up in the world and how I now lead.

~

Almost a year to the day of submitting this chapter to the publisher, I walked away from a role as the leader of a national organization before I started my own consulting practice. I'd been there for eighteen months, three of which were my notice period. This, my friends, is progress.

The organization was not in alignment with my values. The more I learned, the more I saw that we didn't walk our talk, and I felt this viscerally during my tenure. After working with my team, trying to shift the organizational culture, and being shot down at every turn by the company's ownership, I made the difficult decision to leave. During my morning devotional practice, I focused on clearing my conditioning around what it meant to 'quit' and sat with the fear I had around how others would perceive this short stint in what was my biggest leadership opportunity to date.

By the time I gave notice, I knew I had done everything I could in my role to contribute to positive change. It was very hard to leave my team, but I could not stay and support the decisions being made. It was not lost on me that sometimes leadership looks like walking away. My decision signaled others who felt the same. It permitted them to do what was best for their needs, and within weeks of my departure, twenty-five percent of the workforce had left the company.

At every stage of my journey, fear was present. Each time it invited me to look deeper within and notice where I was out of alignment, where there was clarity to uncover. As we meet and clear our fear, we raise our level of consciousness, and our intuition grows stronger. With consistent practice, just like exercising a muscle, we can rely on our intuitive strength to support and guide us. We learn to trust it more than our egoic need to give in to or avoid our fear. We can lead consciously, congruently, and in alignment with our values and beliefs. This path will transform the way we lead, allowing us to bring all of who we are to our life and work.

So, let me ask you, what is your fear inviting you to discover about yourself?

About Sonja

I'm a leadership specialist, Intuitive Intelligence trainer, and principal consultant of The Expansion Practice. I bring a unique alchemy to my clients from twenty years of leadership and organizational development experience, along with a realization that I, like each of you, am deeply intuitive.

In my own journey, I've worked with visionary and textbook toxic leaders and many others who fall somewhere in-between. After a decade of supporting leaders to scale their organization's impact, I have unique insight into the leadership required to navigate and sustain that course successfully. As a result, I'm committed to bringing forth a new leadership paradigm where we live and lead from our highest form of intelligence, our intuitive intelligence, while creating transformational change in organizational culture.

Conscious Revolution

I work with leaders and social purpose organizations that recognize their purpose is far greater than their fear of expansion. Those who have reached a plateau or personal burnout, feeling they've hit the limit of what is possible with their current level of understanding. Those ready to expand their capacity to lead beyond the subconscious fears and limiting beliefs that hold them back.

Find me at:
Website: theexpansionpractice.com
Instagram: instagram.com/theexpansionpractice
LinkedIn: linkedin.com/in/sonjaharvey
Twitter: twitter.com/sonjaharvey_

Krista Hammerbacher Haapala

ALIGN AND FLOW WITH YOUR PLEASURE REVOLUTION

What I am about to tell you, you already know. You may not know it in your cognitive mind, but you know this wisdom in the way you feel at home somewhere. You know this wisdom in how you choose the colors while creating your masterpiece. You know this wisdom in the way you start to sway when holding a baby. You know this wisdom in how you take a deep breath when you behold the sunset.

You know this wisdom because it already lives in you. In fact, this *knowing* is sourced from you, by you, and through you. The essence of *you* is this knowing. It is vast and precious, extraordinary and mundane, sacred and profane. This knowing is everything and nothing in simultaneously honoring dynamic balance with laws of physics that have yet to be discovered.

Our true nature, the infinity within and without, is illuminated by pleasure. This light in many of us becomes dimmed by living in our earthly cultures. We can feel it. We sense that light is under there somewhere. And because it is irresistible, this light shines through even in the darkest times. Often it shines especially in the darkest of times. So, it is wise of us to pay heed.

Pleasure is sustenance. Pleasure is life force made manifest. Pleasure is the path to our dearest and most profound callings. And yet, many of us live in cultures that require us to earn our pleasure, put pleasure last, see pleasure as a weakness, or even perceive pleasure as a threat when not granted by the establishment. It makes sense then that many cultures seeking power, particularly patriarchal ones, would gatekeep and shame pleasure because it's such a potent wellspring of influence.

Often, we're first aware of this pleasure-rationing when we feel in an energetic deficit, whether personal or systemic circumstances cause this. We may find ourselves taking inventory of our lives and wondering what *we* are doing *wrong* to feel so estranged from ourselves, our power, and our joy. The static and dissonance of unnecessary suffering grow too extreme, incongruent with the miracle of existence itself. We start to seek answers to questions that are still vague and cosmic.

Is this all there is?
Why does fulfillment feel so fleeting?
Where is the anchor in this chaos?

For me, the depths of this exploration started as a nebulous dissatisfaction with my day-to-day as a young mother of two sons. I was the flex parent, with my partner traveling weekly for work. We both found our work fulfilling in its own way, yet the life we led seemed to be leading us. Still, like many parents who feel frayed by all the demands, I carried on. Amidst the challenges were the moments of peace and contentment that can become the pillars on which resilience and gratitude are built. These portals to our infinite truth get easily overlooked in life. The profound wisdom of that awareness got lost on me at the time. The core deep need to recognize intentional pleasure as spiritual sustenance wouldn't yet dawn on me until the darkest nights yet to come.

It was in 2013 when my mother finally passed on after defying breast cancer for as long as she could. During our last night together, the night before Mother's Day, she told me to 'be there' for my boys, her grandsons. While we watched the dawning of one of her last days in this earthly realm together, I decided to remove my risk of following in her footsteps by resolving to have a preventative double mastectomy. Later that year, I followed through on that decision. Having that choice was a choice of privilege for which I am grateful. I saw the peace on Mom's face when she felt in her heart that morning I would heed the lessons of her journey.

In the aftermath of grief and surgeries, the estrangement I was feeling from myself and my power seemed to be at bay. A good, solid life-and-death responsibility will do that for the spirit. I had a task, a sacred task, and many things felt hopeful despite the grief and the ongoing healing journey. But as time passed and seemed to smooth the sharpness from the hurt, day-to-day life began to feel day-to-day again. And then again, the flatness, the feeling of deficit, the alienation from the miracle of existence crept back.

I missed an opportunity in this trial, an opportunity to become more acquainted with what felt suppressed, a source of wonder and energy I could tap into, especially when times felt so dark. It was this wonder and energy from easeful and joyous times that I longed for when it was darkest. I took these key things for granted amid the joyous experiences. I wasn't present and mindful to savor and harvest the life force of those times in flow and ease. As I didn't fully embody the learning from the first crucible, it would take another dive into darkness for me to embody the knowing buried so deep inside me under the cultural messaging of controlling and rationing pleasure.

It was 2016 when my partner, my sweetheart since I was nineteen, began having stroke symptoms after a workout at the gym we owned together. I call him my Brironman, a playful combination of Brian and Iron Man since he is both. We learned that this man, a picture of health and vitality, has a rare genetic disorder called moyamoya, which was the cause of his multiple strokes. While in the hospital, we learned he needed life-saving brain surgery to restore the possibility of him learning to talk and walk again, if he survived at all. It was a surprising and shocking circumstance where all we could do was take the risk. I'm grateful to share it was a successful risk. And while my Brironman is still committed to therapy to rehabilitate to his level of peace, he is indeed living life to its fullest, talking, walking, laughing, and loving.

Yet the intensity of such a life experience will forever change you. So, leaving his story to his telling, I share that after my experience at Mom's bedside, I vowed to steep myself fully into the teachings of this wild and unimaginable fate. In the weeks I sat by Brian's bedside, there was only uncertainty and suffering, it seemed. And still, there would be moments of smiles, of connection with our sons, of laughter, of, dare I say it, pleasure.

During the most inimical and adverse circumstances, it was pleasure that we pursued and craved. During these times, those brief glimpses of solace through basic pleasure were my lifeline. Those fleeting moments when I could exhale and connect with the now allowed me to carry on for my whole family. Many might not consider there is any pleasure in those circumstances, but pleasure looks precisely like this in the crucible. It's just a bit more comfort amidst suffering. The touch of a loved one in the direst of times can be a lifeline. The taste of ice cream can be a sanctuary. The pages of an immersive book can be a refuge. A conscious breath can be hope.

In the darkest times, the faintest light can make the greatest impact.

Now imagine how powerful that attention to pleasure can be as an integrated and ongoing commitment to harnessing it as pure fuel, as the life force manifest that it is.

That is my invitation to you. Embody the learning independent from the suffering.

Krista Hammerbacher Haapala

Even if life or fate hasn't dealt you the direst of circumstances, in fact, especially if it hasn't: First, I am grateful! I sincerely desire to share this perspective precisely so that suffering is an unnecessary part of this learning equation. And second, I invite you to recognize all the opportunities you have to truly savor and even amplify the pleasure in your life.

We all experience suffering as a facet of the natural course of this existence. While some may view suffering as the balance to pleasure, my perception is that all experience during this earthly turn is here for our enlightenment. Many ancient and contemporary spiritual teachings support that vantage. That doesn't mean we have to like it! We may have aspects of ourselves that fundamentally object to the concept that all experiences serve our enlightenment. However, consciousness design, the enlightenment approach I employ in my life and with clients, invites us to honor those aspects by listening and *still* aligning with our bliss path.

What is revolutionary is claiming our pleasure through all life's experiences as the sustenance, life force energy, and guidance that it is. Focusing on pleasure itself is a revolutionary act. Ordaining pleasure as valuable in and of itself is radical. Seeking pleasure for pleasure's sake illuminates the true path of our consciousness. To honor this path is countercultural, and you will encounter resistance from the established power structure.

When we recognize who is rationing our pleasure and how ingrained it is within us to devalue and ration our own pleasure, the aha moment may feel stunning, heavy, or even like we have somehow been betrayed or betrayed ourselves. Now is the time to change that, to throw off the messages of pleasure-rationing and embrace the power of our pleasure.

We don't have to live in a 'grin and bear it' environment. When we claim the power of our pleasure, we are sovereign beings who can then model that choice for others. The implicit permission-granting through aligning and flowing with pleasure is the foundation of this revolution. When we start to perceive through the lens of pleasure and even bliss, the world around us shifts. We perceive opportunity where before there may have been toil. We perceive freedom where before there may have been constriction. We perceive peace where there may have been strife.

To make this shift into your own personal pleasure revolution, you will be learning and unlearning simultaneously. We must detoxify from the cultural messaging that there is some official pleasure keeper doling out the pleasure according to who is deserving. That has become normalized for many of us. You earn your vacation time. You pine for the carefree weekends. We clamor for holidays to 'get a break and have some fun'.

So, what about the rest of your life? Who does that belong to? Who do you need to check in with to invite in some fun, pleasure, or bliss? No one. Not a single person but yourself. That is the secret the capitalist patriarchy guards thoroughly. Yet all it takes is choosing to align and flow with your pleasure little by little at first to engage the feedback loop. And when you feel how much more open, easeful, peaceful, and energized your life can feel, your pleasure practices become irresistible.

Remember, this path to pleasure is revolutionary. While we may recognize that pleasure is natural in the course of this life, it's the insidiousness of the controlling messages that quietly cause accumulated harm. Consider when you were a child. For many of us, we can recall a chorus of 'sit down', 'sit still', and 'put that down', translating to, 'Stop doing what is in your bliss and pleasure so you can do what you are told!' As adults, we do have responsibilities, of course. But when we elevate pleasure as a valued principle and align and flow with it, even our responsibilities exist to support our ease, peace, and bliss.

The separation from our bliss is caused by cultural messages, not by following our intuitive wisdom. That is where the dissonance originates—separation from our bliss because we don't choose to value pleasure. When we begin to recognize this separation and trust that pleasure illuminates our path to enlightenment, it brings clarity that often feels 'too easy', as my clients often say. One client shared a sentiment that really shines a light on this awakening: 'I can't believe all along that depriving myself of pleasure is actually depriving myself of guidance on my path.'

That awakening feeling 'too easy' is itself an illustration of how complete the brainwashing is. Why is it true that *life is hard?* Indeed, suffering is a part of life, and it can take a toll, but life is also joyous, beautiful, wonderous, exhilarating, and a fucking miracle.

How do you choose to let that *truth* live and breathe in your existence?

That's where the revolution to create your personal pleasure principles comes into play. When we develop the foundation of our own personal pleasure revolution, we create an inspirational and countercultural manifesto to elevate bliss consciousness. We have a foundation to focus on *instead* of what was handed to us, instead of power and control-influenced cultural dynamic. You create your own proactive pleasure ethic that creates and informs a feedback loop in your actions that becomes self-reinforcing. You feel the undeniable results, so pleasure-led living becomes irresistible. In fact, you may even notice that the environment and the people around you begin to shift due to your example and your vibration. This is a quantum living concept sourced from physics called entrainment. All we are is energy, after all.

The elegance and simplicity of these pleasure principles are that they are unique to you. And as I've already shared, what I'm telling you, you already know deep in your body, heart, and energy. The resonance is an unshakable knowing in your infinite essence. Often what it takes to become embodied in your pleasure practices is an uncovering or an excavation of that essence, a remembering of a no time, no space, no one consciousness state. Your bliss consciousness is always an aspect of the human you.

This expansive unity with the awareness that all experiences serve your enlightenment and are guided by that intuitive wisdom is your *most* core knowing. That knowing is like none other. It is precisely this resonance we must reacquaint ourselves with because that is why we are each here. As

Conscious Revolution

Ram Dass said, 'We are all just walking each other home.' Some interpret this home state as death, the portal back into the infinite. What if home isn't this life's death? What if home is the knowing that we are bliss incarnate?

Might we choose to let bliss into our lives here on this glorious earthbound adventure?

We are powerful creatures born with a blissful wish. Enlightenment through bliss is our charge. Let's use our power to elevate pleasure to its authentic status, a blueprint for your ease and peace. Owning our power as sovereign beings will require we wrest control out of the hands of those who have seized it to keep us complacent and needing to buy what they are selling to rehabilitate our pleasureless lives. That's what revolution is all about, after all.

We are all mirrors and messengers for one another. The bliss and pleasure you integrate into your life serve the collective. Your bliss consciousness shines to show others the way. And it is perfectly appropriate to begin with the Self. Indeed, it is only this facet of consciousness, this one glorious face of the Oneness, that we get to direct. Hold the power of living your pleasure as the sacred vow that it is, a commitment to your enlightenment following the most joyful path. Embody your pleasure, and others will follow.

Joining together and recognizing this energetic shift in the collective consciousness will not come without resistance. A revolution requires a steadfast promise to Self to stay the course, to overcome resistance, to embrace this life as a practice, and to, again and again, turn our hearts to the light. And what a magnificent invitation to practice self-worship and get more and more intimate with elevating pleasure with each choice.

Invite yourself to become aware of *one thing*, simply the *one thing* in each moment or circumstance that will bring you closer to living your pleasure. As you do, the bliss unfolds before you, and you can't believe you ever forgot the truth of what you are—bliss consciousness incarnate. Welcome home.

About Krista

I serve the collective as a consciousness design leader, author, and pleasure activist. I bring my embodiment of the pleasure-illuminated life into my retreats, circles, books, and art. I love to write, and I'm the author of books including *Unlearn Moderation, Body 2.0, Ischemia, Conscious Revolution,* and the forthcoming *The Bliss Talks: Find Your Edge Through Pleasure-Illuminated Living.*

Since 2005, I have been honored to guide visionaries to create their own pleasure-illuminated, enlightened lives and loves. Through my radical consciousness design movement, I dismantle the patriarchy through pleasure activism so all can flow in their relationships to Self, Source, and the humans in their world.

I serve humans who intuitively feel there is a dimension of bliss just beyond their reach and are aspiring to invite pleasure to illuminate their

Conscious Revolution

path. Those who are restless and feel the heaviness of cultural pressures to please, behave, or conform find both provocation and inspiration in my offerings. My circles, retreats, and sessions are created for those ready to catalyze their energetic shift from the usual to the euphoric in all they do, those called to find their edge and live their bliss.

I find my own edge and bliss as a collage artist as well as through meditative devotion, hiking, dancing, crosswords, weightlifting, and wandering in my RV. My practice spans the planet, and I live oceanside, a few steps from the Maine Woods.

Find me at:
Instagram: instagram.com/theblissmystic
Facebook: facebook.com/krista.writes

Enisa Cuturich

MY JOURNEY TO UNLEASH ENISA

Firstly I want you to imagine the feeling of holding onto massive cement blocks, starting off with one, then each year on your birthday, you're chained to another and another and another. Until, twenty-six years later, you're completely numb to the pain because you've learned how to disconnect from your emotional body. You're exhausted from holding onto the blocks that weigh you down. You're convinced that something must be *seriously* wrong with you because it doesn't seem like anyone around you is as exhausted or chained to cement blocks.

With your twenty-seventh birthday fast approaching, everything in you tells you that it's just not worth it. There is no way you can possibly go on and add another cement block. So you decide that the only way to be gifted freedom finally is to turn the self-harm into suicide.

But then something greater than you, something within you, sends you a very clear and critical message that scares the fuck out of you. It actually scares you more than taking your own life. The message is to do something you've never thought to do before because you've never seen anyone do it. It's something you were told time and time again not to do because it's unsafe, wrong, painful, and going to fuck up everything you've built over the last twenty-six years. You will be judged and seen as weak.

The message is to *unleash* from the cement blocks.

Take the ultimate leap of faith into the unknown and reconnect your emotional body so you feel the weight gift you with the natural reaction to *let go* of the blocks and be free.

This is what it means to *unleash* and choose to be a part of the conscious revolution. It's to set yourself free.

My journey to Unleash myself started when the mask I wore started to suffocate me. It was a mask that showed the world a confident party girl who was there for everyone, would drop anything for her friends, worked hard in a job that people were impressed by, and had her shit together. Nothing fazed her. She could take anything the world threw at her.

She spoke of her trauma as if it hadn't affected her. Like it was no big deal. She allowed people to say things, do things and take advantage of her because *she didn't care*. Nothing shook her. She was strong *all the time*.

That girl who was chained to these *huge* blocks of sadness, anger, shame, heartache, abandonment, guilt, and fear, and the pain was all covered in thick solid cement that just seemed to be getting bigger, thicker, and heavier as each year went by.

You see, the girl built up a long list of roles, responsibilities, and expectations that she allowed others to put on her because she taught them how to treat her, what to expect from her, and who she believed she needed to be to feel loved and to feel like she mattered.

Here is the truth behind the mask.

I was born into a family that came from generations of trauma and abuse. My mum was held hostage by my father in an abusive domestic relationship which meant that my home was always full of chaos. Daily yelling, screaming, banging, police being called, tears, and fear. This led to me growing up holding myself hostage to feelings of being unsafe and chaos, meaning I found those environments and people more comfortable than when I was safe.

My childhood gifted me many incredible lessons and talents, like my powerful AF intuition and ability to read, know, and understand human behavior and triggers. I developed this from a place of survival and fear of setting off my father. I could read his mood from when he woke to when he entered the door. Understanding his moods told me what kind of day it would be. I intuitively knew how many drinks until the monster would come out to feed, and I observed what triggered certain topics and people. I also picked up a lot from my mum in the same way. When we were on our own, meaning when mum finally left him, I'd read my mum's moods and triggers in the same way.

This is something I'm beyond grateful for because it's become my superpower to support the healing and transformation of women's lives worldwide!

But this also taught me to alter who I was to keep the peace, not to trigger people. I was taught not to be my fullest, brightest self at a very young age because it was unsafe.

The truth is that living in survival mode and low-vibrational states is all I knew, hence the cement blocks. I believed that being your fullest, truest self was unsafe, so much so that I constantly questioned and doubted myself, constantly repeating, 'I don't know what I like. I don't know what I want,' and even, 'Well, I don't really know who I am.'

I didn't trust myself, people, and situations or environments that made me feel good or have a high vibe because I was convinced that something would go wrong, I'd be punished in some way, or it'd be taken away.

Hello! to a life of playing small, people-pleasing, disconnecting from my emotions and me, and not allowing people to get too close, feeling lost, like something was missing or something was wrong with me, comparing myself to others, not feeling good enough for anything, and not feeling worthy to walk the earth.

Take note here and feel into what I am about to share because this is huge!

I was feeling all of the above, *but* I still had this deep desire for *big* things, meaning I could see there was more to life. I could see happy people around me living their lives, and I deeply desired that. I've also never wanted anyone to feel as shit as I felt, so my desire to help people and make an impact was always there.

Because I know that we can feel all of these huge emotions and heaviness, but there are moments we don't, like when you are taking a poo, for example, or whenever it may be for you when you aren't at the peak of what feels like a breaking point.

Let's keep going.

I fell in love with dance and wanted to be a professional dancer with all my heart and soul. *But* I allowed other people's opinions and society's programs of what is normal and achievable to influence me to abandon my dream. I constantly sought validation from others, convinced I didn't know who I was. I allowed people's opinions, both good and bad, to create my identity, which caused *more* inner chaos. You could never tell, though, because I had been playing my role in everyone else's movies so well, meaning everything they needed me to be, I was. Both hero and villain.

While in my own movie, I was reenacting the generational trauma cycles just with different characters, so I was experiencing the same sort of abusive relationships, self-loathing, self-abandonment, and self-sacrifice, working in nine-to-five jobs. Really though, it was twenty-four hours a day as I was fighting for freedom in life the only way I knew how, the only way I was taught how. Which is making a fuck ton of money by working really hard and sacrificing your happiness for however many years you can have freedom.

But when I got to the point where, honestly, I was convincing myself that suicide was the only way to gain freedom, I had to *unleash* from the blocks and take a leap of faith into the unknown, which was scary because, well … it's the unknown. I had no fucking idea what was going to happen!

So the first block I had to *unleash* was my pride because, from what I was told and experienced, asking for help or support was a weakness. It meant admitting something was wrong with me and I wasn't okay, and the fear of judgment by others was at an all-time high!

But I was done feeling empty and struggling, and it shook me that I truly didn't want to be on earth. I never fully attempted suicide because I didn't want to put my mum through more trauma than she had already endured.

The catalyst to *unleash* me was saying yes to an incredible online wealth creation opportunity that lit me up. This might be hard to understand fully or a bit like 'What the fuck!' but hear me out.

It was a *massive* stretch for me. The investment, the way I would have to show up as the fully expressed version of myself, and the judgment I had of making money online at the time. It may sound crazy, but saying 'Yes!' to creating a business online completely transformed my relationship with self, family, life, love, and money!

I didn't know that investing in myself in that way gave me all the lady tingles for life again because I had *finally* been shown *how* to create the freedom I was desperate for. I didn't know what it was actually gifting me.

Something that no one can put a price on, *fulfillment and community*.

Saying yes to creating legacy wealth, which was outside the *normal*, allowed me to surround myself with a community of people all talking about personal growth and connection. They talked about moving through life, leading with who you truly are, sharing your story, dreams, and wisdom with others, healing, and following your intuition.

As I write, my heart expands again because I found my tribe.

I became part of a conscious conversation and introduced myself to people who were not only living the life I desired but showing up unapologetic and fully expressed.

They weren't afraid or ashamed to be who they were, to share their trauma, challenges, and wins. That level of inner freedom is what I desired for myself, and these incredible humans were and are so willing to hold a safe and supportive space for me and others to do the same.

I fell in love with the journey of falling in love with myself, so I invested and continue to invest in coaches, mentors, and practitioner training to support me in breaking the generational cycle of trauma, self-abandonment, and self-sacrifice.

I'm continually healing, learning, growing, connecting, and *unleashing* my Divine Goddess Self, so I can be who I now know I was destined to be. The soul-lead leader and facilitator of the journey to *unleash* women's wealthy, wild, and free selves.

Plus, be the imperfectly perfect mama to my little man Luka, who fuels my passion for living an unleashed life! Why? Because by accepting all parts of myself and choosing to devote myself to my true soul mission and desire and it will cause a ripple effect for him to know it's safe to be one hundred percent himself, imperfectly perfect.

By me owning and sharing the lessons of my fuck ups with love, compassion, and empowerment and knowing that it's all happening for me, I've shifted my perspective. I'm practicing patience and understanding of others because I believe with all my heart that it is our birthright to live a wealthy, wild, and free life while fiercely loving every part of ourselves unconditionally, which is why I have devoted my life to unleashing humanity.

It doesn't matter where you come from, your past trauma, or your environment at any given moment. *You* can decide to transform your life. You are more powerful than you know.

You just have to be willing to invest in yourself and get comfortable with being uncomfortable. This means feeling all the fear and doubt but doing it anyway, knowing that whatever is on the other side is perfect for you. It's all happening for you.

I want to gift you three keys I discovered along the way that supported me to *unleash*.

Trigger warning! You may want to scream at me, call me a fuckhead, or go into the ultimate defensive mode where you want to legit punch me in the face because you think I am a *C U Next Tuesday* and to that, I say, 'You're welcome!'

Lean into that feeling and ask yourself, *What am I scared to admit at this moment? And what are these feelings really about?*

You're not fucking broken, and stop saying you are!

Gorgeous human, *you are not broken*. You are more powerful than you think, and all the answers you need are not outside of you. They're within you.

Your parents, childhood environment, experiences, friends, family, the things you watch, ex-lovers, teachers, and society have all, dare I say it, brainwashed you. They've brainwashed you into believing that you're less than others, that you're limited. They've made you feel guilty or greedy for wanting more. They've told you money is the root of all evil and rich people are assholes that have made you not want to be one. You've been told your worth is based on what you do, not on who you are.

And guess what? It's all bullshit!

You are not broken! There is absolutely nothing wrong with you! In fact, you are motherfucking magical, and at any given moment, you can decide to claim your power and change your life. Period.

You are what you say you are.

So the more you say you are broken, the more you will feel it, embody it, and be it.

So here is a small journal exercise to bring awareness about how you feel about yourself and your life.

You can do these around each key area of life!

Conscious Revolution

- Relationship with self
- Relationships in general, whether it be lovers, friends, or co-workers
- Family
- Career
- Health
- Money
- Personal growth

Journal prompts:

1. Give them a rating out of ten. Ten being fucking amazing wouldn't change a thing, zero being beyond shit. Then write out your reason for the rating, what emotions come up for you, negative self-talk, feelings in your body, memories, and people related.
2. How do you want to feel about this area? How would you like to be experiencing this area? What would make it ten out of ten? What would have to happen to make it a ten?
3. Re-read the above and take notes of everything running in your mind telling you that this or that will never happen for you. Any limiting beliefs, emotions, or people's voices you hear telling you that you can't have the thing.
4. Now, ask yourself if any of that is one hundred percent true. Notice here that none of it is fucking true. *No one* has carved it in stone somewhere that any of the above is true!
5. Now rewrite your story by disproving all the limiting thoughts to beliefs that fucking serve you!

I'm a powerful human. I'm a magnet to my desires. I AM (whatever it is you are).

Note: if you have some funky emotions, that's amazing. They are coming up to be cleared. Feel free to reach out if you need support clearing them.

'Change your story, change your life.' – Tony Robbins.

I love this quote because it is so true! No one is coming to save you!

So many of us are waiting for something outside of ourselves to change before we (insert any desire you have for yourself here). We're waiting for people to tell us what to do or for people to change something about themselves.

'When my partner stops drinking, things will get better, and I will be happier ... when my mum finally tells me she is proud of me, then I'll feel worthy ... I only feel good when people tell me I'm good.'

Or we're just waiting for things to show up without doing anything to make it happen, like manifesting winning the lotto, but you aren't willing to buy a ticket.

Are you ready for the truth bomb? You want to be saved!

You want Prince Charming, Fairy Godmother, Shrek, Wonder Woman, or whoever it's for you to come and save you from the reality you feel stuck in, that you feel like you need to be saved from.

Here is where the bomb drops ...

No one is coming to save you because *you*, my friend, are the hero of your *own* story. When you're in the early days, wearing a blindfold, unwilling to see your light, the universe, God, or whatever you want to call it will send you signs, and here is how you see them and save yourself.

When you hear something that immediately sparks a little tingle within and makes your ears perk up—it's a sign.

If you're watching someone speak and you find them magnetic, or they trigger you in a way that doesn't repulse you but may feel a little like a roll of the eye 'easy for you to say' kinda vibe...lean in, listen more, and reach out.

Start to take note of how certain people, places, and things make you feel. Your body and energy don't lie. If you feel drained AF after seeing certain people, that's a *huge* sign of where to start to shift things. If you're lit the F up by your job or even a certain task in your job, take note and do more of it.

Ask for guidance. Ask your spiritual team. The universe, God, and angels are all there waiting for you to ask them for guidance, so here are your steps:

1. Pull your journal out and sit in a clear space with no distractions. Somewhere you feel safe.
2. Take some big, gentle breaths to center yourself and close your eyes. Say this aloud, 'God (Universe or whatever source you want to evoke), I'm ready to receive clear, obvious guidance around (whatever you need support with). Thank you so much for being with me today. Ready and willing to support me. Allow me to receive your messages clearly, and in a way I can fully understand. I'm ready to see things differently. Tell me what you would have me do.'
3. Open your eyes and write without judgment. Whatever comes to you, write it down, and don't stop writing until you intuitively know you're done.
4. Then go back and read it. You'll get exactly what you asked for. If you are new to this, it will feel funny at first, but stick with it. Practice it often, and it will get easier and easier. Like anything!
5. It's not easy, and yes, you may want to run.

They don't call it inner work for nothing! It *is* work. You have to get comfortable being uncomfortable!

I'm not going to lie to you. Like anything you learn, choosing to *unleash* can feel scary, and sometimes it can be hard. Yes, you will stumble, fall, hurt, laugh, cry, have fun, and win, but the more you choose to lean in, the more you choose to practice, the easier and quicker it gets because you become a master.

There have been *many* times I have wanted to run, yes, I mean actually run away from some things, *but* here is the gold.

That is a sign that you're about to have a *huge* breakthrough and clear some massive stuff that will allow a *quantum leap* in your life!

I always see clients who say to me, 'I didn't want to see you today.

I felt so much resistance,' or, 'It took so much for me to jump on the call.'

And my reply is *always* the same! 'FUCK YES! You are about to have the most life-changing session.' Because our unconscious mind is there to keep us safe, but here is the thing, how we're operating today, with all the trauma, the emotions, behaviors, and patterns that aren't serving the old limiting belief systems we have about ourselves, life, relationships, money, and people are all fucking us up!

Your unconscious mind believes that it is SAFE because it doesn't know any other way because for (insert your age) years, you've been operating with all that and haven't died.

So, when we do something new, like release all those old, shitty programs and start to do the new thing, like install the new program, our unconscious mind is resistant to it because it doesn't know it's safe yet.

That's where all my gentle, profound, and life-changing processes come in to support the unconscious mind to know that it's safe and it can let the old go and welcome in the new.

That's why it's *so* important to get comfortable and even excited about being uncomfortable or feeling resistant to the work.

Okay, so what do you do if you want to run? Here is what I do. I ask myself these questions and repeat this mantra.

1. Am I safe at this moment? The answer is always yes!
2. What emotions are coming up for me, and what am I scared of? For me, it's usually shame that I've been holding onto something that surrounds a part of myself, my life, or fear of admitting how I feel.
3. How will it continue to impact my life if I don't face it now?

Then I remind myself of my why, I remind myself that it's safe to love myself, and it sounds like this ...

'I am Enisa fucking Cuturich. I was placed on this earth to support women in living a wealthy, wild, and free life by unleashing their truest,

Conscious Revolution

fullest selves. I am here to lead by example by leaning into fear, shame, guilt, and judgment to unleash myself from it. I am here to live a wealthy, wild, and free life for myself, my son, and humanity so I may show them what is truly possible. I allow myself to love myself unconditionally, to expand my heart by fully accepting who I am at this moment, and honor the woman I am destined to be. It starts here. It starts now. I've got this.'

Allow yourself to feel into whatever mantra feels good for you, feels expansive and loving. An added bonus for you.

My clients come to me because they desire to successfully *unleash* from the judgment of others and live a free, fulfilling life, which they can see I have embodied.

The truth is when you choose to start living a conscious life, let's call it choosing to join the revolution, you do set yourself free. You *unleash*, which means accepting, owning, and choosing to love all parts of you, which can and will trigger people because of their own trauma, shame, and limiting mindset.

It has *nothing* to do with you.

You have one fucking life, and you don't want to get to the end of it regretting not living it to the fullest.

I love you all and can't wait to connect with you.

About Enisa

Hey Gorgeous Humans,

Enisa here, international Unleash facilitator, wealth creation mentor, international number-one bestselling author, mother, lover, daughter, sister, friend, and human. I support people to unleash who they are at their core, to set themselves free from fear, shame, guilt, trauma, and anything that isn't serving their divine truth. What does that really mean? It means I support you in being the fullest, most aligned, and most powerful version of yourself by guiding you on a journey of discovery, self-acceptance, self-love, and deep healing.

I am a multi-passionate multidimensional being who is gifted in helping people Unleash their vision of a wealthy, wild, and free life. I started my journey by saying yes to partnering with an incredible company that allowed me to create legacy wealth by leveraging their amazing products within the direct sales space. For anyone who hasn't jumped on the Kangen Water train, I highly recommend you do, as their water ionizes are the best in the world and have completely changed my health and wealth. Jump on my website for more info.

But that was really the catalyst for everything for me. I spent the next few years deeply healing myself, becoming an NLP master practitioner, master in hypnosis, master Family Freedom Protocol practitioner, relationship sovereignty expert, trauma healer, intuitive practitioner, and business mentor. I am devoted to my mission on this planet which is to unleash humanity and raise the frequency of the planet by unleashing the divine feminine goddess energy within women.

Why am I so passionate, and why do I love the work UNLEASH?

Well, I came from generations of women who were held hostage to the story that women are less than. They were abused in every form possible. My life was going down the same path, but I made a promise to myself that I would be the cycle breaker, and I have been.

I've seen what unhealed trauma, self-loathing, self-abandonment, self-sacrifice, self-harm, and self-abuse can do firsthand, and among many women around me, I refused to allow that to be normal, and I refuse to pass that down to my children.

So, I UNLEASHED myself from all of that. I use the word unleash as the feeling of healing, personal growth, and owning your power, so you feel free. The heaviness, struggle, and the suffocating feeling we can feel when we are powerless to life goes. You unleash all of that, creating a deep level of faith in yourself and something greater.

Other than all of the above, my number one role is mama to my beautiful son, Luka, who I'm obsessed with. I love dancing, singing, having deep conversations with friends, and going on retreats, as honestly, I'm obsessed with personal development! Currently, I live in Bali with my partner and son, but the wealthy, wild, and free vision now is to travel the world full-time, seeing it all.

Enisa Cuturich

Find me at:
Website: unleashwithenisa.com
Instagram: instagram.com/unleashwithenisa
Facebook: facebook.com/enisaeccuturich

Nila Matthews

AWAKENING FLOW WITH CONSCIOUS CREATIVITY

'Bring forth what is within you, for it will save you.' – *Gospel of Thomas*

Consciousness is always creating and runs deeper than your thinking mind. Creation is all that is and the source of all: the universe, innovative breakthroughs, the creation story, and your creation story. Creatives are special as they use neural pathways differently (Kaufman, 2013) and are thirty-seven percent happier when in flow. So the question is: What are you creating? What is the depth and quality of your creations? Do you have the courage to create, and what is your relationship with creativity?

I ask because creativity saved me and is a reflection of our lives. My work products have won awards, but this is deeper. Creativity ignited a passion and life force energy that stopped the need for my seventh major operation and pulled me out of helplessness in a self-collapsing conscious world. I ask because your approach to creativity and the characters you meet in this process reflect your creative output and your life, energy, and relationships.

I invite you on a journey to meet creative characters in the hope of liberating and removing the energetic drag that may lessen your creative energy and flow in life. This map shares the framework of creativity to navigate the creation or creativity pool. It can help you travel from the shallow end and unlock neuroscience and nervous system secrets. However, more specifically, it can help you understand the vagus nerve, our resilience nerve helping master ourselves to the magical deep end. It is risky for our brain to create anything new (Kotler, 2021), yet our evolution, chosen or not, demands change, so Chaos enters our creation party.

A dysregulated nervous system places a break on this process, leaving us stuck in the middle, repeating life problems or old ideas. Harnessing the power of your creative spirit can help you find ease in navigating yourself to the middle. From the middle, we can flow to the deep end, where the magic happens. Control and process are substituted for ritual, navigating our brainwave states, and changing our energy signature that calls our higher expansive consciousness. From here, courting creativity and inspiration is easier. Suppressing our creativity not only limits our ability to leave our gift, legacy, or dharma in the world, but having no creative release leads to stuck-ness, ill health (something I know well), or worse, scarcity mentality. This, I believe, is the route to most jealousy, fear, and othering and stops not only your flow but the creativity and flow of others. This serves no one.

So, are creatives special?

Yes. In the ancient world, creativity was felt to be bestowed to only a few by gods, maybe because they were honored with time and space to create. The Greeks called creation a 'discovery'. Today we know creative brains are different from ordinary people. In a study conducted by Adobe in 2012, it was found that creativity is the critical skill most successful CEOs display. Enlightened minds possess this, and creatives are thirty percent happier (Kotler, 2021). Having worked, studied, and been fascinated with the process and minds of creatives, I believe we can all be creative by cultivating a creative mindset and connecting with our own energy and passion. Psychologists have found that being open to experience is the only personality trait consistently linked with creativity (Chamorro-Premuzic, 2015; McCrae, 1987), so finding an opening and changing perspective are critical to moving forward in life and when creating.

CONSCIOUS CREATIVITY: EXPANSION OR CONTRACTION

The term and definition of creativity are hotly debated. Simonton (2000) calls it 'optimum human functioning'. This reflects my wider use of the term, including big-C creativity and little-c, everyday creativity or problem-solving. Psychologists often talk about it as a 'process of bringing into being something novel and useful' (Sternberg & O'Hara, 1999).

Useful depends on the context and intention, especially when judged through the lens of business or culture. However, it could be 'useful' as it saves lives. The study of creativity in America formally occurred because of curiosity about creative pilots who survived and saved lives in World War II (Barron & Harrington, 1981). Alternatively, it could be useful because it releases you from the grips of a downward spiral.

That was me in 2016, hiding under my duvet, feeling done after my sixth major operation in four years, two late pregnancy losses, unconscious trauma and shame, and sidelined at work for my ongoing treatments. Then I got an angry phone call from a friend, telling me to get out of my own pity party and call her. She cared!

I laughed when that call woke me up after the shock wore off. Then I did what Hermione Granger from *Harry Potter* did, and I do best; I turned to books. Or more importantly, I permitted myself to get creative to find a solution. This helped expand my concretized heavy thoughts, which dragged on energy. Then I researched, and as I gave positive energy, energy gave back.

Energy has become my superpower, but granting self-permission is the critical ingredient that many creatives, like Anthony Davies, the Group

Creative Director of Sky, said can hold people back. Permission without self-blame started the release process and helped me find my passion for helping others. My chaotic journey led me to give up my corporate job for a master's in psychology, brain scanning studies, and a journey through somatic, the science of intuition and spirituality. Novelty blended out of chaos.

Were my decision and process easy? No. My intuition was screaming at me, but I suffered from indecision and wasted energy. I had commitments and fears, so I waited until a bad conversation at work before I left. I know now that my unregulated nervous system blocked my inner knowing. Even on the new path, I was left looking back, anxious and not surrendering. I let Chaos frustrate me and anxiety squeeze me without proper armor or tools. Now I come prepared with a line of defense: a creative, courageous, compassionate mindset looking for an opening and tools for the moment of a squeeze. It is a daily practice.

INTRODUCING THE CHARACTERS OF CREATIVITY

I introduce Chaos, Anxiety, and Flow as characters to help unpack the human creative process.

Chaos is our evolution, dressed as the antagonist. The Greek god Chaos, or Khaos, emerged as an element from an explosion at the dawn of creation, thus essential to creating something new (Khaos, n.d., para. 1). Creativity can be explosive and frustrating. However, our evolution is on the other side of our comfort, so embracing chaos and uncertainty means befriending fear. The elephant-headed god Ganesh can help us understand fear as a friend or messenger.

Ganesh, the god of beginnings, whom Hindus pray to remove obstacles and fears, ironically places them in our path so we can evolve. So, as he courageously rides his fear of mice or sometimes said to be rats, we too should ride fear and ask, 'What would you have me know to improve?' The answer: break open and let go of all you know.

Conscious Revolution

I have shed tears over bad grades at university, the shame of losing babies, and bad jobs. Sitting in this uncomfortableness is where most of my shifts and breakthroughs occur, and your own tears are healing. Chaos has asked me to evolve, ask for help, or move on, as it was not meant for me. The suffering happened because I added shame, but as my intuitive, somatic teacher, Elisha Halpin, says, 'What are you available for?' Not shame!

Anxiety, unlike the adrenaline of stress, which can add fuel or friction to act, anxiety's role is to drain energy. I think of Anxiety as the slippery cousin of Khaos. It watches for our weaknesses and then offers our fears and shadows to strain our nervous system and inject shame, making me/us feel small, stuck, and sabotaged. My usual shadow archetype (Myss, 2006) is the saboteur. The other critical ones are child, victim, and prostitute. This momentarily numbs me as I fill my angst with food, drink, anger, or freeze, then fills me with shame and regret. Still, my body talks to me, my stomach gets knotted, and my shoulders get tight as fear plays at the level of physiology and psychology. I now pay attention because they are my signs to see that saboteur is looming, and they are enough to remind me that I am not available for shame or regret.

I believe flow is the outcome and an active process, unlike passively going with the flow out of resignation. It is defined as an optimal state of being and consciousness by psychologist Mihaly Csikzentmilay (2013). However, flow is a term understood in ancient wisdom as critical to awakening and intuition, an inner knowing from within and also non-locally that's available to us all.

A report by McKinsey (2013) found that a flow state increases strategic problem-solving by 500%. In *The Art of Impossible*, Steven Kotler (2021) states, 'Flow is the brain on creative overdrive,' where attentional systems are entirely absorbed and focused, time slips away, and people, including surfers, artists, and meditators, have said to experience oneness.' Flow is a feeling that had followed me all my life like a red thread leading me to my soul essence, even before I was conscious of the science of flow. Flow is openness and energy expansion, where purpose and passion are intrinsically linked to a healthy sense of self, mastery, and intuition. From here, as the ancients did, we can invite and court creativity with, for example, the Greek Goddess of Flow, Rhea, or Goddess of creativity, Saraswati, the flowing one from the Hindu pantheology, or the alchemist within.

THE CREATIVE PROCESS

Many writers on creativity, including Mihaly Csikszentmihalyi, author of *Creativity* (2013), claim creativity has four key cognitive processes.

(i) Preparation (ii) Incubation (iii) Illumination (iv) Verification

Note: The scope of verification is too large to be covered in this chapter.

The stages vary. For some, preparation for illumination may take days, while for others, it takes months. Gladwell (n.d., as cited by Galenson, 2013) differentiated between conceptual creatives and experimental creatives. Conceptual creators like Picasso are younger and tend to know what they want to achieve and create. Cezanne, an experimental creative, made many iterations over months and years, and Galenson noted that they tend to be older. Leonardo Divinci's *Mona Lisa* is said to have taken over sixteen years. I am of the latter group; it is frustrating but fun when I remind myself to have fun. I intuitively know I am onto something, but I need to engineer incubation to bring it out.

Given my experimental approach, self-compassion and insight into the process and the nervous system have prevented me from giving up or from getting burnout. It is important because the nervous system is approximately thirty-four miles long and the holder of stress; it does not differentiate between creativity, work, or life stress, and your brain is in a box (Eagleman, 2016) waiting to be told what to think of itself. Inflicting self-hate due to perfectionism, comparison, or taking on all negative comments from others is harmful, raising the chance of ill health and lowering the energy you bring to your creations and yourself.

Conversely, if you are a fast, conceptual creator, working with different types, viewing them with compassion avoids unhelpful judgment. Knowing yourself and your shadow is important as it impacts your relationships with others and how you sustain your energy. People in flow can be productive and creative but single-minded and intolerant of being disturbed. Yes, I have had to apologize to my family often. I call it a flow rage. Even the Goddess Sarasvati's focus on mastery is said to have led to divorce whether she chose it or not. Your style of creativity should not be a source of loneliness or censure.

THE THREE NEURAL NETWORKS OF CREATIVES

Creating something novel and useful happens at creativity's preparation, incubation, and illumination stages.

Creatives' brains, unlike normal people, use network co-activation to create: It allows a dance between the executive attention network—preparation and avoiding repetition suppression (Brant & Eagleman, 2017, p. 16), which means seeing new in the old; the default mode network, also called the imagination network (Kaufman, 2013); and finally, the salience network. Interestingly, the first two networks cannot come online simultaneously. Instead, the salience network, the noticeability network, via the dorsal anterior cingulate cortex (ACC), sees the patterns, joins the dots, and pulls the thread together. It flips the switch between the two allowing us to solve a problem, illumination. However, the ACC requires one thing to ensure it can function optimally: a good mood.

In hindsight, my laughter after my friend rang helped me switch gears. Neurobiologically, lightness helps the brain ease from high-beta, a brainwave state associated with stress, similar to being stuck in second gear. Creativity cannot happen here; your brain needs to get to an alpha state, or third gear. I call this the alpha bridge to the imagination cell created by alpha or theta brainwaves, then, possibly, to an aha moment by activating a gamma state, given certain conditions are met (Dawson, 2020, p. 130).

We can do this in several ways, including guiding our consciousness into deeper intuitive states, which meditators have done for years. Creativity, I believe, is a journey to and through your intuition, but we can all do it.

Nevertheless, having turned myself into a human lab, I believe we cannot bypass ourselves to generate a good mood for a sustained time, and, more importantly, we will not get past the middle of the pool. I share some tools to show how I do this, but first, I help navigate the shallow side of the pool by developing the right mindset and using some hacks.

Optimizing the individual networks:

The preparation phase of creativity requires your higher-order executive attention network to come online.

Preparation here means researching and using new or past skills but looking with new eyes. I love exploring new things and concepts and listening to new people, which helps me make connections in novel ways. However, at work, it can be seen as rebellious and unnecessary: not staying in my lane. I've learned to become an unapologetic innovation rebel but timebox exploration if a deadline looms.

Some brain areas used in this network include working memory, a pattern prediction, and error detection network, and areas that regulate attentional systems. To effectively create, we need to focus on flowing and being comfortable with not seeing the woods for trees. Setting a firm intention for your creative effort at the start of your creations also helps. Your why is your north star. It should have a strong, meaningful intrinsic motivation for you. It should be a purpose greater than you, to show grit and determination as recommended by creative experts like Amabile (Amabile & Collins, 1999; Amabile & Hennessey, 2010). I write my *why* down as a physical cue, then simplify it to one word. For example, flow and paint it on a stone. When I waiver, it reminds me why I'm playing with chaos.

The executive network allows for creative cognitive hacks, like the remote association test that requires you to find a fourth word associated with these three words: rat-blue-cottage (Mednick, 1962). Or the consequence test asks you to 'Imagine what might happen if …' (Guildford, 1954). Both are basic creativity hacks, but I apply them to my life situation and dreams. But here, I'll explore the three *B*s of creativity, bend, break, and blend (Brant & Eagleman, 2017). It forms the basis of most creative endeavors.

DIVERGENT THINKING: A CREATIVE MINDSET

There is an illustration in the children's book, *The Little Prince* by Antoine De Saint-Exupéry (Antoine, 1943) that the book's narrator shows to any 'interesting' adult, hoping they see the world differently. Most adults saw a hat and told the child to stop drawing when told the truth. Only the Little Prince saw what it was: A boa constrictor digesting an elephant!

The image has stuck with me. It is genius! Firstly, it illustrates how creative children and people can stop being creative due to the negativity of others, wanting to please them, or fearing groupthink. However, the Little Prince is doing divergent thinking, showing cognitive flexibility.

Scientists measure this by looking at four characteristics: fluency, flexibility, originality, and elaboration of ideas. However, the magic for me is the invitation to change your perspective. Psychologists know there is no one perspective. Perspective comprises your upbringing, beliefs, unconscious biases, values, or even what color you just saw. To be creative, we can bend to create something new. Claude Monet's picture of the *Rouen Cathedral* is the same image painted in a different light. Perception is both malleable, cultural, and subjective.

The Muller-Lyer visual illusion of the two lines appearing to be different lengths is not a worldwide phenomenon, surprising western scientists. Cross-cultural studies found that only Westerners consistently fall for the illusion (Brant, 2017, as cited in Henrich et al., 2011).

Nila Matthews

The Muller-Lyer Visual illusion

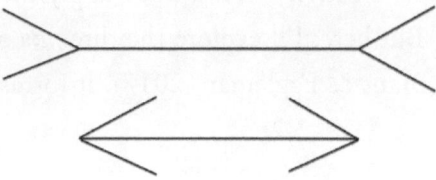

Image Replicated by Nila Matthews

Is a change in perspective that powerful? *A Course in Miracles* (ACIM, 2007), a spiritual text, defines a miracle as a change in a perspective and asks, 'Can you see this differently?' If you are challenged. Can you bend? Psychologist and astronomer Dr Michael Lennox often says in his podcast *Conscious Embodiment*, 'It's not your first thought that counts. It's your second,' (Lennox, 2022). So I try to breathe, get perspective, and then speak.

SPACECRAFT APOLLO 13'S EXPLOSION DEMONSTRATED BREAKING

NASA needed to create an air purification system with plastic bags, cardboard, and tape. Running against time, it was the classic 'let's work the problem, people' (Entrepreneur, n.d.). With limited tools, they did not just need engineers; they needed calm, creative engineers. Breaking and blending the items in a new way led to something new and useful that saved lives. My service is now a blending of science meets spirituality meets a sense of lightness.

THE IMAGINATION NETWORK—INCUBATION TO ILLUMINATION: 'WHAT IS DEEPER THAN THAT?'

Einstein (1929) said, 'Imagination is more powerful than knowledge.' Creatives like Freeman Dyson and Newton have claimed that mind wandering or incubation time often preceded a breakthrough (Csikszentmihalyi, 2013; Kounios et al., 2008). Einstein was famous for his thought experiments and for playing his violin to help solve problems. Or, more aptly, letting his subconscious solve the problem.

The default mode network (DMN) is a large hub of connection that spans various brain regions (Buckner et al., 2008; Jung et al., 2013) that can impact this. Limb and Braun used fMRI brain scanning techniques on six full-time jazz musicians improvising on the piano. The scanner showed that the DMN was activated and is essential to the creative process (Limb & Braun, 2008), but the prefrontal cortex (PFC) quietened, quietening the self-critical brain. A great imagination fires the DMN into expanded consciousness, always creating, so it creates great things. However, this is not always the case.

However, Dawson Church in *Bliss Brain* (2020) calls this region the Demon Network, where 'belief bullets' could shoot you down if you have not mastered your mind. Beliefs inform our perception and the permission we give ourselves in life and in creativity. I believe life mirrors our FAB—feelings, actions, and beliefs. If unchecked, this can create false perceptions and could limit us.

When my daughter, Eloise, was eight and nine, she was nicknamed Squeeze, and ironically, Chaos loved to squeeze her. She started an art project for a regional competition. With seventy percent complete, she made a mistake, cried, and threw it in the bin. In quiet horror, I took it out and hugged her, calmly breathing, a technique called co-regulation with pranayama breathing (*prana* equals life and *ayama* equals control). Eventually, we laughed about something, and she began again. We were shocked when Eloise won the competition. Had I told her off, or she stopped there, her belief may have shot her down, never putting herself forward again. At that moment, she was a mirror of my younger self. The belief bullet that I was backward, not good enough, learning to read late as we moved a lot, and I became the wallflower at school to avoid being picked on as the brown girl/other. I did not put myself forward; when I did, it was only my logical head muting my creative feminine power.

However, creativity and intuition are feminine powers. Unleashing this has been my biggest edge as I rejected the feminine when I was young. She represented a weak, domesticated, obedient, does not argue, or cantankerous woman who needed to use her guiles to land a rich husband. My first small rebellion against being a good girl was refusing to learn how to cook as my brothers weren't expected to, which I now regret. I felt it was safer being masculine at home and in corporate life. Later in life, my operations around my feminine parts, or the sacral-creativity chakra, further muted this.

I have needed to give myself permission to connect with all the parts of me. I am not the only one in this patriarchal society who has muted this divine shakti, creative power. But on this path, my consciousness has been liberated by new intuitive sisters, who, like 'women who run with the wolfs' (Pinkola Este, 2009), have shown me the creative force and beauty of the feminine, whatever feminine means for them: to be wild or a goddess, a warrior or an alchemist, a pleasure-seeking mystic. They are all the faces of creativity and shakti. I lean into the discomfort of chaos that asks me to open to my feminine. I use creativity to peel open, one layer after the other. It is painful and beautiful, uncomfortable conversations ensue, and things are falling away and coming together. However, I surrender with ease and sometimes creative anger, but always conscious that I am releasing stuck energy and awakening to my wholeness. I bend, break, and blend.

To lead a creative, unapologetic life, I have invoked the power of Kali. The masculine tradition would have us believe she is a blood-sucking dark goddess. Yet, in the liberated right hand of tantric tradition, *tra* means to expand, and *tric* are the tools to liberate or expand (Kempton, 2013); she is a liberating force in our life, consciousness, and ability to create something new. Borrow her daggers with respect as I do, to cut yourself from limiting FAB that will drag energy down and stop you from shining in your fullest expression and creating the life and legacy you are meant to. But be warned, she finds you.

So, how fab is your FAB? What do you need to unlearn to see your creative feminine power? The alchemical saying in the Taoism and Hermetic Law (2017) of Correspondence state, 'As within, so without, as above, so below,' (Three Initiates) is key, meaning that life mirrors our inner world. Even if your FAB is not great, creativity can help find an opening, heal or shift dense energy.

Energy is important because the law of vibration from the Hermetic laws (2017) states we attract back at the vibration we resonate. I am taking time to deal with the below and entrain my energy. The law of thermodynamics tells us energy cannot disappear, so we must transmute it by first acknowledging our fears to allow that energy to transmute to a lighter form. Energetics is a fuller discussion covered by the science of consciousness and authors like Dr David Hawkins (2020). However, know that your words, coupled with feelings, are like powerful spells and have energy that are good and bad. So use them wisely.

ENERGY LANDS: TRAUMA IS DENSE, STUCK ENERGY AND EMOTION

The Latin word for emotion is *emovere* to move out. Bessel van der Kolk's book, *The Body Keeps the Score,* caught my imagination (Bessel, 2015). He claims that people in trauma cannot be creative. However, he and other somatic experts suggest embodied movement and creativity may be the key to healing their trauma. Dr Eugene Gendlin (Gendlin, n.d.), after a decade-long study, found that patients who start to sense and feel *into* their bodies had a better recovery rate. This is backed by the findings around the vagus nerve, which show that vagal toning techniques, such as pranayama and movement, can help us heal, thus helping us dip our toes into the creative pool (Embody lab, 2022).

In the book *When Shadows Fall* by Sita Brahmachari (2021), her main characters work through and release trauma by unconsciously using creative expressions such as liberated primal movement or art. Something I resonate with to help shift Chaos. I did this when he entered my life after my operations and do it now during creative blocks, fear, or when I feel stuck. Using creative expression and energy tools like tapping to change my energy signature and flow.

I believe there is a symbiotic relationship between creativity and chaos. When chaos enters our life, we can use creative expression to meet it and regulate ourselves. When chaos comes to creativity, know it is there to evolve us, and we can use tools to ease our system.

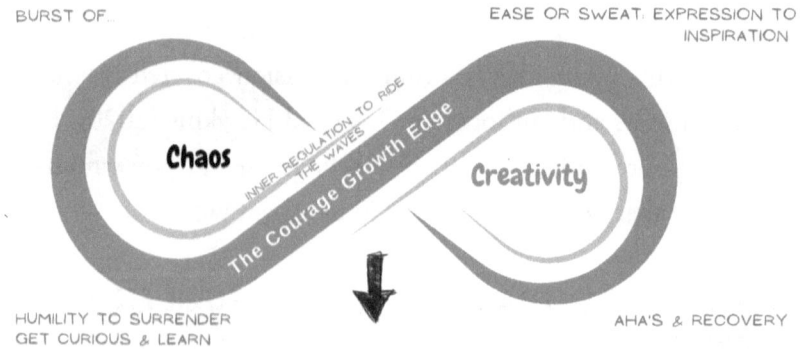

Symbiosis: The Flow Of Creativity & Choas

Original by Nila Matthews

INCUBATION ENGINEERING: OPTIMISE DMN AND FLOW

Experts suggest encouraging the DMN to take a break and focus on non-demanding tasks (Baird et al., 2021). This could include counting blocks, doing a jigsaw, or anything you enjoy for as little as five minutes. Looking out the window and letting your mind wander on the expansiveness of the sky and the universe or looking at green landscapes or scenery allows an opening. After I was bedridden following my operations, looking out of the window across the blue skies and following the red kites catching thermals and flying to their nests high on the horse chestnut trees helped me escape and recover.

Ritualizing anything and everything, for example, a jasmine tea ceremony, shifts my energy signature. This is essential to court my default mode network (DMN). I run, cycle, and walk the dog but make it sacred. I dance so that I may lose myself; as Kotler (2021) says, it allows us to befriend our anterior cingulate cortex (ACC). Author Sita Brahmarchi said, 'Doodling, daydreaming, and sleep are essential to help pull the thread of [her] books together.' Sleep naturally takes our brain wave states into the theta, a place where we can be more creative and reprogram our brains if done right.

To clear energy, I also use the fire of breath breathing, leading into a self-guided meditation, which is optimal for crossing the alpha bridge. From here, relaxed and releasing expectations, it is easier to flow, be in a good mood, and channel writing with an uncensored stream of consciousness. This invites the salience network to come online.

THE SALIENCE NETWORK

There are many different components within this one neural network. Still, the salience network is about noticeability, possible only if we are in a good mood. I offer a method that has been highly researched as a simple gateway to flow. So we take a detour from the brain to the heart. Be warned, my creative flow is a downpour, so I invite you to prepare your recording device or journal and get organized so you do not get overwhelmed.

HEART COHERENCE: GETTING TO THE DEEP END OF CREATIVITY AND INTUITION.

My brain scanning studies showed that the unconscious knew before the conscious caught up, but the HeartMath Institute's (HeartMath, n.d.) research has found that the heart knows five seconds quicker if emotions and the mind are bought into heart-coherence. How? Simply place your hand and attention on your heart.

With the intensity of feeling, focus on feelings of gratitude, appreciation, or joy, lighting a spark in your heart (Institute of Intuitive Intelligence, n.d.). To heighten this, add loving music and surrender, breathing the glow around to and out of your body and to your energetic body. Let it expand. This method employs ancient wisdom, focusing on the anahata heart chakra, or portal of your inner knowing, your intuition. But to flow, the masculine Shiva and creative feminine Shakti energy must dance equally.

While writing this chapter, I felt the usual chaos and heaviness. I sat in deep meditation and was reminded of a piece of channeled writing that came to me in 2021. It was about creating the ultra-verse, blending creativity and healing as the alchemist. I did not know what it meant. In this present session, as I crossed the creativity bridge, I saw a pool, the shallow end, and the deep end. A beautiful, energetic presence said, '*You're dipping your toes in—heighten your energy to go up to the ultra-verse. From there, write for me: I am Saraswati. From heightened energy, you will flow, heal, and create.*' This method is about changing your energy signature to create at a higher level. And this is what I now offer others: awakening the genius alchemist in us all.

My point is that your energy and flow matter to the quality of your life, creations, and consciousness. Every day I meet my fear, shift my energy (don't worry, it gets easier), and cultivate gratitude by seeing everything with curiosity, which, neurobiologically, allows me to befriend my ACC and my intuition to open. My creative mindset or spirit has shifted my perspective and found an opening that allows me to be curious, accepting, and forgiving rather than be in heavy, stuck ill energy, which was my narrative for so long. Plus, my higher vibrations help me find ease and flow to cultivate connections. I attract and create playfully and purposely, trusting that my path will unfold just as it's meant to. The good news is

Conscious Revolution

that as we release control of the form and outcome, it is in our control to create and step toward the life we want.

As Picasso said, but with my little amendment, 'Inspiration ...' and energy '... will find you working.' The world needs more curious innovation rebels with a purpose. Just believe, play, and flow with gratitude.

About Nila

Helloooo and welcome, beautiful soul. I love meeting new people and trying new things. Yes, I'm truly curious, adventurous, and passionate. Yet, sometimes, life's challenges can mute innate qualities and can also mute joy, energy, and intuition, which happened to me. I've realized that I'm here to help people turn these positive traits up, as I did for myself. Over eighteen years, I've led and created many award-winning technology innovations for corporates as a behaviorally informed product specialist. I'm also a volunteer mental health tutor and run a local miscarriage support group called Pebbles Story, and I'm an Intuitive Intelligence trainer. I'm now the founder of Awakening Flow, training and coaching people to gain energy mastery and create from their soul essence and inner power.

However, my new path began after my sixth major operation, two late miscarriages, and feeling dejected and resigned. I felt small, stuck, and sabotaged by the shallow side of life, my creativity stalled, and I was close to burnout, something many of my clients also face at the start of their journey before they create the life and legacy they are here to create. On my journey to find solutions, I left my corporate job of eighteen years and returned to university to do a master's and brain scanning studies, following a traditional psychology route. Then I found myself on a path of energy and trauma healing, somatic, and science of intuition, realizing nothing changed from the level of the mind alone. With multi-modality tools and creatively blending disciples, my passion, joy, health, inner creative alchemist, and intuition began to flow. Intuition is a gift we all have and can train, taking any endeavor and life to the deep end of the creativity pool. I want to train others to flow, moving past unconscious blocks.

My service is science meets spirituality, meets a sense of humor and technology wrapped in goddess mythology. The flow methods and tools I use have shifted my consciousness, energy, and work because they help regulate the nervous system and reset neurobiology and self-limiting behavioral programs. My mission is to revolutionize how women and businesses approach well-being and trauma recovery.

I firmly believe that when we are in flow, shining in our zone of genius, power, and joy, we fulfill our legacy compassionately, allowing others to do the same. This means avoiding a scarcity mindset that holds ourselves and others back. Instead, we avoid burnout and befriend Chaos to overcome our limiting fears with a higher energy signature.

I am grateful daily for my loving friends, family, my daughter who helps me be a child and grow up all at once, my dog Dobby, my running buddy, and my bike for helping me sweat it out and flow.

Find me at:
Website: awakeningflow.com

Nila Matthews

Instagram: instagram.com/nila_awakeningflow
LinkedIn: linkedin.com/in/nilamatthews
Email: info@awakeningflow.com

Ash Moreland

WHO AM I?

'I can't do this anymore!'

It was June 2020, during the first year of the COVID-19 lockdowns in Melbourne, Australia—the most locked-down city in the world. I was in a state of total defeat, desperation, and exasperation.

If you were an observer looking in on my life, you would've seen a 'successful' woman. I had two beautiful kids, a partner I loved, a modern home, a successful career with a six-figure salary, and even my dream car. I had everything the worldly 'recipe' for success called for. But what you *wouldn't* have seen, despite all of these ingredients for 'success', was that I was dead inside. Numb.

Lost.

Disconnected.

Totally and completely unfulfilled.

This can be triggering for society. There was a time before I had all of these things when it was triggering for me, too. This perception that somehow if you had these tangible assets or accolades, you're less entitled to suffer. Thoughts like, *They have it all. What more could they possibly want?* I chased happiness, which always seemed to be just out of reach. I thought that maybe I'd feel happy when I ticked the next box. Yet, I never was. So, what was wrong with me? I felt deeply ashamed that I had 'all of this', yet it still wasn't enough to make me happy.

Given the state of the world at that time, it would be easy, and even socially acceptable, to blame COVID-19 for some kind of 'mental breakdown'. Yet, the twenty years of therapy and multiple suicide attempts and ideations leading up to that moment pointed to a very long history of suffering. This suffering was independent of who I was in a relationship with, where I was working, or what car I was driving. As much as I had a pattern of blaming anyone and everything around me for how I experienced life, the only common denominator in all of my suffering was *me*.

I had always run my life on autopilot—rushing, worrying, panicking, perfectionism, unrelenting standards, always escaping the present moment with 'busyness' and any form of numbing. If truth be told, these characteristics probably resulted in my supposed success in the first place.

As a child, I learned if I swallowed my emotions, even if they were ready to burst from me, kept quiet, even when my spirit yearned to be loud and free, and followed instructions without questioning, even if they didn't make sense to me, if I achieved top marks in school and won BMX events, I was a 'good girl'. This taught me a lot about who I was and who I needed to be in order to be loveable or even tolerable.

I skipped grades in primary school due to high academic achievement and subsequently moved twenty-three hours away from my family when I was sixteen to start university. I studied a double degree full-time and worked up to three jobs where the pay was barely $14 an hour to fund my life. I graduated with a high-distinction average, with offers in various programs fully funded via scholarships. I eventually chose to continue studying in an honors and PhD program specializing in neuroplasticity.

I began lecturing during my honors year at the age of twenty and had my first full-time gig in academia by the age of twenty-three. Without a doubt, this autopilot mode and the belief that if I was the perfect 'good girl' I learned to be in my childhood, then I was safe, most definitely launched me into 'success'. However, there is one fundamental flaw with this paradigm. By virtue of being human, I'm *not* perfect, so I was never safe! Doctors labeled this perceived unsafety as anxiety and depression, an eating disorder, and ADHD. But what if 'I' wasn't anxious or depressed? What if these traits and behaviors that 'I' exhibited weren't even 'me' or 'mine'?

The truth is, these labels became embedded within my identity. They didn't just describe an experience I was having or portray something I was doing. They were nouns that I identified as. They were 'me' and 'I' them. Other nouns I identified as were mom, partner, teacher, colleague, daughter, sister, and friend. Who 'I' was had *literally* been reduced to which label I was at that moment.

This created constant existential crises in my life because any time there was a threat to any one of those *nounified* versions of me, my mind perceived it as a threat to my very existence. For example, it wholeheartedly felt like my fault if a friend became distant, even if it had nothing to do with me, and this threat to my identity resulted in me spiraling into a dark place because if they weren't my friend, I felt like I was losing part of my 'self'. In this version of reality, I was. In toxic relationships, I'd abandon myself rather than risk losing the relationship because that relationship was also part of who 'I' was. My kids yelling 'I don't love you!' when I wouldn't let them eat lollies for breakfast triggered 'me' because their approval and being a 'good mom' was as important to my identity as my right arm. So, losing that validation was perceived as a threat to my very existence. To safeguard all of the labels and roles that made me 'me', I developed a whole charade of masks and facades to people-please and be 'good enough' to be worthy of connection. However, the greater the web of masking became, the more lost and disconnected 'I' felt.

Eventually, I began to question—what if there was more to 'me' than just Elijah and Elodie's mom, Wayne and Jenny's daughter, or the teacher of hundreds of students at uni? What if 'I' wasn't who I thought I was?

How exhausting trying to be a hundred different things to a hundred different people! Of course, I'm not a thing, and my identity is more than a noun. The problem was, if I looked beyond these labels, these nouns, I had no idea who 'I' even was. I didn't know what I liked. I didn't know what I needed. I didn't even know how I felt about things. But if 'I' am not these things, who am I?

Who are YOU?

This concept unraveled over time and then finally landed. The revelation hit me like a ton of bricks. Have you ever been so drunk that you're pretty much passed out, and someone either abruptly kicks you or throws cold water to 'wake you up'? That's what this moment was like for me. It was like snapping out of some television drama where I'd been playing the lead character of a person unworthy of love, undeserving of connection, and living a fabricated truth, reaching an absolute breaking point.

At that moment, something awakened in me. A fire within ignited in response to a posture of surrender the moment I proclaimed, 'I can't do this anymore!' I experienced the real 'me' for what felt like the first time. The me that is more than flesh and bones and more than labels. My *soul* self that's connected to all that is. So, at that moment, I thought 'I' either had to crash and burn *or* 'I' would rise up like a phoenix from the ashes. It turns out, it was both. It meant the death of the worldly constructed self, the product of all the labeling and distorted structure of reality, and the uprising of the eternal self and an awareness of the ultimate *Truth*.

Over time, I realized that I had been unconscious almost my entire life. I only saw what my biases carefully filtered through in the physical realm. This ensured I remained obedient on the rat wheel of life, distracted by consumerism and chasing the ever-unattainable commodity of 'happiness'. A life of duality based on endless judgments from the programming deep within my unconscious mind. Good versus bad, fat versus skinny, hot versus cold, right versus wrong. For me, like many before me, it took an absolute crisis, a real sense of emergency, to squeeze me to my spiritual 'emergence'. So here I was, a spiritual awakening—a regaining of consciousness.

So, what is consciousness, and why do we need a revolution?

Consciousness is everything, everywhere.

It is infinite.

It is you.

You are it.

Yet, it is not limited to the physical you, but the eternal you that exists beyond time and space—your pure source energy, your soul. Consciousness is often used synonymously with awareness. While they are related, they are not the same thing. Awareness is a product of our attention, allowing us to know or perceive situations and facts. When perception, which is a construct of the mind as a response to our experiences sensed by our physical body, and consciousness, a spiritual phenomenon, are aligned—that is, when our thoughts, actions, and behaviors align with what we ultimately know to be the greater good—we can be very intentional in our response to whatever stimulus we face. For example, our responses are borne out of love, kindness, compassion, and gentleness, even in challenging situations. From a nervous system perspective, this promotes regulation and safety, which is only possible in the absence of a perceived threat or inner conflict. However, when our perception and consciousness are misaligned, and our identity strays further and further from our true soul-self, our nervous system detects threats, even if there's no actual threat, and becomes dysregulated. In this state, our consciousness is often dissociated. At the extreme level, it can result in depersonalization or derealisation. Our spirit or soul is so disconnected from the body that we don't even recognize our physical state as ourselves. When operating from UNconsciousness, our thoughts and behaviors are like automatic reflexes. These reactions happen rapidly regardless of consequence, they're often exaggerated, and they're generally operating like a program to keep us safe—if [x], then [y]. Sometimes these reactions are productive and helpful, yet other times the reactions are dysfunctional and destructive.

To further differentiate between consciousness and perceptive awareness, how many *E*s were there in the last sentence? What was the number plate of the car you followed the last time you drove? What type of earrings did the cashier wear at the last shop you were in?

The reality is you probably can't answer these questions. Even though these details were available to your consciousness, you were not instructed to pay attention to them, so your mind did not gain awareness of them. This demonstrates a limitation of the 'body' component of our being. Because of an information processing bottleneck, we can only 'cognitively' allocate attention to a couple of hundred bits of information every second. So, it is human nature to remain oblivious to a huge portion of our existence.

Our brain constantly filters out huge volumes of information deemed irrelevant or unimportant simply because we lack the availability of neural resources. For example, suppose our unconscious mind stores a program that values brand names. In that case, we will preferentially allocate attention to the details of brands from the sea of infinite data in our environment.

If we're programmed to believe we are unworthy of love, we will pay attention to the insignificant imperfections in our body, our character, or any aspect of ourselves to the exclusion of everything else. If we are programmed to believe we are not good enough, we will preferentially give attention to and possibly even get stuck in rumination over seemingly irrational or inconsequential things like forgetting to pick up bread on the way home from work, making a simple mistake while cooking dinner, or not receiving a text reply from someone we care about.

Yet, we've excluded the infinite bits of evidence in our environment every single day that shows us that we *are*, in fact, worthy of love and good enough. Reread this!

This programming tells our brain what to focus on—and as they say, where our attention goes, our neural firing flows. Consider the exploitation of televisions, radios, and other means of broadcasting our inherently perceived unsafety and a system of centralized governments exercising control over national and global activity while censoring and suppressing anything contradicting a specific narrative.

Our minds have been manipulated via mass hypnosis to preferentially filter fear, pain, and suffering into our awareness by focusing on various flavors of crises and tragedy, perpetuating human suffering, and propping up an economy that profiteers off war, pain, hurt, and control. Mass compliance is gained through molding unconsciousness towards a preferred bias and exploiting the human drive to avoid fear and punishment. Shakespeare said, 'There is nothing more confining than the prison we don't know we are in.' And UNconsciousness and distorted mental programming is the prison society has been in.

As a neuroscientist, I understood the brain. Yet, even after years of measuring parameters and behaviors of the nervous system in response to various stimuli, it had never occurred to me that in no anatomy textbook and no images from any form of sophisticated scanning device was there such a thing as a 'mind'. Further, I had never been taught what 'mind' or 'mental' meant in my ten years of university studies, *many* years of therapy for mental illness, or the time spent studying human behavior. This was interesting to me, given that 'mental' health is often reduced to brain dysfunction. Yet, despite having the greatest access to medical care and resources, rates of mental illness in society have never been higher. That's because 'mental' is defined as relating to the mind, *not* the brain.

So, in my quest to understand results I couldn't explain in the physical, despite all the science and tools at my disposal, I began to explore if the anomalies and outliers I saw in studying the brain were because of the influence of the mind. After all, we are body, *and* mind, *and* spirit, but I had only been 'measuring' the body.

As I journeyed, I got to observe my own mind. Interestingly, the more I focused my attention on my mind, the more I gained control back, and it seemed to hold less power over me. As my mind opened more and more, I started receiving messages and information in different forms, from visions, to 'inner knowings', to messages literally like someone was 'speaking to me'. A thought reached my awareness, but I *very* strongly knew that it wasn't 'my' thought that entered my mind. I was repeatedly challenged on this spiritual journey with many things that resonated and felt like answers. But there were more questions for each answer, and nothing really hit like a full embodied *knowing*.

I was historically very triggered by religion and uncomfortable with the term God—I preferred Universe. Yet, as I understood more about my mind, or so I thought, and my intimate personal relationship developed with the created (the Universe and everything within it), I began experiencing the fullness of the creator. Pure source of all that is. I was intuitively guided to read the Bible for the first time in eighteen years as a spiritual text, rather than the belting stick of indoctrination and dogma that it had been in my early life, which led me to 'make up my mind' about religion. With this different perspective, and the opening of my mind, the words brought life and revelation into my awareness.

One verse hit me as only a supernatural revelation can, Mark 12:31 (ESV, 2008). After explaining what commandments are the most important, Jesus responded, 'Love your neighbor as yourself.' This one verse in the Bible spoke to me and exposed so much of the programming in my own mind that was the root of my suffering and distorted identity.

When I read that verse, my neighbor was excruciatingly painful, and soon after, another neighbor attempted to break into my home! I realized it is very easy to love a fun neighbor who is quiet, who mows your lawn, brings in your bin, and bakes you treats. But let me tell you, love was the *last* thing I felt for my neighbors. I may have even thrown around the 'Hate' word as they were barbecuing and partying only meters from my bedroom window, as usual, at 3 am, just moments before I promptly stomped out there in my dressing gown to express in no uncertain terms my utter dissatisfaction!

This stemmed from a hardening of my heart and distortion of my mind that put conditions on when I could or could not love another. So, let me ask: Would *you* still ground into deep love and acceptance, maintaining peace in response to a loud, messy, aggressive neighbor, or even a criminal? What about if you learned they were a pedophile? What is the limit of your conditions to experience love for them?

During COVID-19, vaccination status and political views became the limiting condition for many, resulting in families being torn apart. What conditions are you placing on loving *your* family? Your friends? Your children? YourSELF? What assumptions are you making right now in your mind about what it means to actually love another? Is it inviting them in for tea? Is it making sure they're always happy? Is it sending them a Christmas card? Our mind is responsible for the meaning we assign to things, and that meaning feels so real, but this is the deception.

This commandment's second dimension of complexity is what is meant by 'yourself'. To love my neighbor as myself requires me to know who I truly am *and* assumes that even if I do know my 'self', I'm capable of loving that self well. How many people do you know who love themselves well, in soft-pure love and acceptance, rather than ego? If you see someone loving themselves, what comes up for you? What did loving 'self' look like? Was it bubble baths? A round of golf? Was it wearing expensive accessories? Furthermore, what meaning do we assign to people who love themselves? For me, it was stories like 'they're full of themselves' or 'they think they're better than everyone else'.

Seeing someone love themselves was very triggering for me, so how could I actually love myself while vulnerable to the judgments I made about others? See how this one Bible verse offered complete exposure of my utter state of UNconsciousness, showing so much distorted meaning-making of the world, and highlighting the identity crisis I was in? All this time, it was the state of my *mind* creating suffering, which the worldly things around me had influenced.

One of my gripes against God was if he loved me so much, how could he allow me to suffer? Yet, suffering was not God's doing! Even the story of creation itself explains that we were made in the likeness and image of God—our soul state of pure consciousness is love! Our suffering was man-made. *My* suffering stemmed from developing my identity and understanding of who 'I' was (and who I was not, as a young child from the UNconsciousness of my loved ones, governments, institutions, religions, pop culture, media, and many other influences.

So, hopefully, it's clear by now that it's our UNconscious mind, adopted during our formative years from all of the worldly influences around us, that automatically applies worldly value systems, groupings, divisions, classifications, judgments, and morality to every person, situation, and circumstance. It deceives us by preferentially allocating attentional resources to specific things that offer us a distorted sense of reality and identity.

Our identities are grounded in nouns established as by-products of our early life experiences, but this is not who we truly are! These identities, by default, lead to opposition and division in a dualistic world. For example, you can *either* fit into a category called 'I am a good mom' or 'I am *not* a good mom', each of which is very separate from the other and relies on judgment. As a result of these unconscious judgments, our world is experiencing war and conflict within families, schools, nations, and beyond.

When we *unbecome* everything the world led us to believe we were or weren't and become grounded in the Truth of our pure consciousness, our soul-self, it brings rise to the you that is infinite and whole exactly as it is. It is pure existence with a totality of self that starts and ends with 'I am'. For the soul-self, there is no opposition and nothing you're not, only what you are.

It's inclusive, expansive, and connected. It invites pure, unconditional love through absolute acceptance without judgment. Imagine how different our world would be when everyone in it can exist in pure consciousness! A world where no one's state of being is dependent on anyone else, and we can exist in pure harmony. Interestingly, harmony in the context of music doesn't depend on all musical notes being identical, but rather it is the coming together of differing notes in unison simultaneously. We don't *need* people to share the same perspectives, values, morals, beliefs, or viewpoints as us in order to live harmoniously. We simply need to coexist even with our differences from a state of pure consciousness.

So, where does all of this leave us regarding a conscious revolution? The word revolution literally means a forcible overthrow of a government or social order in favor of a new system.

1 John 4:4-6 (ESV, 2018) tells us, 'You, dear children, are from God and have overcome them, because the one who is in you is greater than the one who is in the world. They are from the world and therefore speak from the viewpoint of the world, and the world listens to them. We are from God, and whoever knows God listens to us; but whoever is not from God does not listen to us. This is how we recognize the Spirit of truth and the spirit of falsehood.'

The social order to be overthrown here is the drastic state of UNconsciousness of most of humanity—the 'self' that is identified in the world. It requires the full removal of the veil of deception and falsehood over society that's made us believe this distorted reality of who we are, what requires our attention, and how we're disconnected and different based on what nouns we do or don't identify as. Instead, we see with absolute clarity the Truth of our oneness, our connectedness, and our worthiness of love. The new social order is revival and the Spirit of truth. We must literally bring consciousness back to life.

The Bible tells us in Colossians 3:8-15 (ESV, 2018) to achieve this, we 'must also rid yourselves of all such things as these: anger, rage, malice, slander, and filthy language from your lips. Do not lie to each other, since you have taken off your old self with its practices and have put on the new self, which is being renewed in knowledge in the image of its Creator. Here there is no Gentile or Jew, circumcised or uncircumcised, barbarian, Scythian, slave or free, but Christ is all, and is in all. Therefore, as God's chosen people, holy and dearly loved, clothe yourselves with compassion, kindness, humility, gentleness and patience. Bear with each other and forgive one another if any of you has a grievance against someone. Forgive as the Lord forgave you. And over all these virtues put on love, which binds them all together in perfect unity. Let the peace of Christ rule in your hearts, since as members of one body you were called to peace. And be thankful.'

If you're not well-versed in biblical history, the emphasis on the nouns or groupings that divided populations during the time that this was written is highlighting that this separation is in the flesh only, but Christ is eternal and exists in us all. But we're not human beings in the flesh having spiritual experiences. We're spiritual beings as souls having human experiences. Galatians 5:22-23 (ESV, 2018) tells us that, 'The fruit of the Spirit is love, joy, peace, patience, kindness, generosity, faithfulness, gentleness and self-control.' These things are not conditional on what we do or don't have, what noun categories we fall under, what we look like, or what we've achieved in the flesh. They are the promises of our existence if we come alive in Christ and return to consciousness.

So we know what consciousness is and why it is so important, we know that UNconsciousness is the root of our suffering, and we know that a revolution is needed, but how? How do we UNprogram the collective mind? First of all, notice the sources of the programming. Media is defined as the main means of mass communication (broadcasting, publishing, and the internet) regarded collectively. There is a reason these things are called 'programs'. To UNprogram our minds, we must start by bringing consciousness and awareness to the media we consume.

Be discerning about what you watch, read, and subscribe to. Even bring awareness to the songs you listen to and the conversations you have with those around you. Be intentional and highly selective about your focus of attention and bring it back to loving your 'self', as we were guided to by Jesus. Self-love starts by recognizing your soul identity that was made in God's image. 1 John 4:12 (ESV, 2018) says, 'No one has ever seen God; but if we love one another, God lives in us and his love is made complete in us.' Just a few verses later in the book of 1 John, it's written that, 'There is no fear in love. But perfect love drives out fear, because fear has to do with punishment.' When loving our 'self' becomes the focus of our attention, fear and punishment become the white noise filtered out of our awareness, and the product is unity, safety, and connection.

Finally, commit as a matter of absolute urgency to doing the deep healing work required to release all past pain, trauma, belief systems, distorted value systems, and unresolved negative emotions at a conscious, unconscious, cellular, spiritual, and energetic level so that you are free to love others unconditionally as you love your 'self', regardless of their human behaviors or conditioning. The most beautiful legacy of all for me as a parent of young children is that if we as a collective of adults in this generation do this work, our next generation of humanity inherits this transformation of renewed minds, and as a result, a renewed Earth. There is no greater mission and no greater army, so let's make it happen.

About Ash

Hi, I'm Dr. Ashleigh Moreland! I'm a highly energetic and passionate neuroscientist, bestselling author, speaker, lecturer, therapist, and consultant on a mission to impact the masses. I grew up in a small country town in Queensland, Australia, and moved solo to Melbourne at sixteen to pursue my academic career.

With a heavy academic focus since 2007, I subsequently completed my PhD in neuroplasticity and built a highly successful career recognized for excellence across teaching, research, and leadership. While still research active and primarily supervising PhD candidates, my focus and passion have shifted to helping people on a large scale to overcome barriers to being present and connecting with themselves and others through awareness, education, and trauma-informed transformation.

This passion became a serious and urgent quest for me after having my first child in 2013 following a severely traumatic birth experience. My child went on to develop significant emotional, mental, and neurodevelopmental challenges. After being dissatisfied with the opinions of various medical experts, I put my academic skill set to good use and became hyperfocused on learning everything possible about healing from a holistic mind-body-spirit perspective.

Becoming a single mother of two following four pregnancy losses and the dissolution of my marriage in 2018, I was forced to dive even more deeply into extreme ownership, self-responsibility, and personal and relational healing. These experiences and significant further study and practitioner training armed me with expertise on psychological, biological, and neurological drivers of behavioral and relational experiences in children and adults alike and tools to change them.

Now remarried and surrounded by fulfilling and nurturing relationships, my kids are happy and healthy. My life is enriched by using my knowledge, skill sets, and lived experience to impact individuals, couples, families, and workplaces worldwide. I partner with people to transform their relationships with themselves and others, enhance performance and productivity, and achieve deep connection and presence through nervous system integration and regulation.

Find me at:
Website: drashleighmoreland.com
TikTok: tiktok.com/@dr.ashleighmoreland?lang=en
Facebook: facebook.com/dr.ashleighmoreland &
Facebook.com/BigPeopleLittlePeopleAU
Instagram: instagram.com/dr.ashleighmoreland

Samantha-Jayne Love

MY CUP IS FULL

And with the snap of my fingers, I'm fully awake.

If only becoming more aware of the world and my place within was that simple.

My journey, like many others, hasn't been one of sunshine and sparkles all the time, though there's been a lot of glitter and laughs throughout my years.

This is a story of how I found myself.

For most of my life, I wanted to fit in, so I'd people-please, bend over backward, and go beyond when my body and soul were saying, *NO!* From delving into training, I now know this is a trauma response.

I didn't know what boundaries were. It's not something we're taught when we're little. Unfortunately, it was many moons ago that society forgot what it was like to have boundaries and to honor them both for self and others. Though having strong boundaries and a strong sense of self is what

Conscious Revolution

I want to be able to show my girls. I called my two beautiful angels into my life because I believed they would fulfill me. I will return to this point later.

I want to show them that you can keep hold of who you are by having consistent boundaries. Then, when they want to change what a boundary looks like, my girls will know how to have a conscious conversation with other people about that change. If that person is unwilling to be okay with these new boundaries, maybe that person is not supposed to be in their life. I know this is what I'm bringing into my life now, knowing where my *yes* is and then knowing and sticking with my *no*.

No is one of the shortest words in the English language, but for some, it's one of the hardest to comprehend. If your body and soul say no, listen. If we don't listen to our innate internal monologue, we do ourselves a disservice. Some would call it our intuition, a gut feeling. However you want to describe it, it's your soul talking to you, guiding you on what steps to take next. And yes, sometimes those steps are challenging as they take you away from your comfort, security, and certainty, even if what we know as comfortable is doing the most harm to us.

Therefore, we go against our own comfort, no? It's so that we can fit in.

My longing to fit in, be liked, and be loved was so great that I forgot how to love myself deeply and unconditionally.

Welcome to the box belief system:

I believe that if we want to fit in, that means going within the box. This box is a societal box that isn't meant for everybody. The box means doing and behaving in a certain way so you don't stand out, but you fit and are loved, safe, and secure. For example, moving around a lot when I was younger, I learned very quickly to act like a chameleon so that the kids would like me. I even attempted to be a circle. Though I'm not a circle or a triangle, I'm a heart. I'm a love heart. I am love.

Yes, yes, I said a heart. That's what I am. I will not fit within a shape on a page or within something. I'm ultimately a big, squishy, glittery, rainbow-colored heart.

Samantha-Jayne Love

I'm not everyone's cup of tea, and that is okay. It's taken me a long time to know that it's okay. In this world, we need all sorts of shapes. If you look at the intricate shapes within a sacred geometry picture, there are so many lines and different shapes.

Being so loving, I really felt that it was my job to make everyone feel happy, and when you do that, you end up exhausted. The life gets drained out of you because the person that you forget to tend to is *you*, and *you* become so unhappy. So consequently, I became comfortable with my heart shape and learned to have a deep love for myself.

When I was a young girl, I'd go on family caravan trips with my gramps and granny. My gramps sang in the choir, so we would sing along to all the songs. I remember this one so vividly, *Running Over, Running Over*, by Seth Sykes, which Granny would start.

These words stayed with me and saved me on many occasions. Although as I've grown, the meaning behind his words has deepened.

When I first read this song growing up with Christian-patriarchal grandparents and Lutheran-matriarchal grandparents, I was under the assumption that the words meant that when someone outside of me, external of me as I believed the 'THE LORD' to be, he would come to save me, that's when my cup would run over. The song always fills me with the most amazing memories. There was laughter. There was cheekiness. There was fun. There was joy, love, and sparkle. This sparkle was from the soul of my grandfather and could be seen in my gramps' eyes.

When I began to break down the song's meaning, the concept that I needed somebody external to myself to make me feel happy, to make my cup full, didn't sit well with me. This really did detrimental things to me. I was looking for somebody to love me so my cup was full. I really looked in all the wrong places. I was never alone. I've always had a partner from the age of sixteen. Even if it wasn't a committed relationship, someone was around. I tried to be the best at all things. This included toxic behaviors like alcohol, drugs, and unsafe sexual practices so that I could fill up my cup. Even a cup filled with toxic waste was a full cup. Consequently, the more I tried to fill it, the emptier it got.

And then I had to learn that the only person who could totally fill my cup was me.

This is where the process began to start finding how to love me. It was a big task, especially as I'd always externally filled up my cup.

Now let's break it down!

What is my cup?

Well, I used to believe it was the human fleshling bag I resided in. Fleshing is not an endearing term; it means a creature made of flesh, a human being devoted to sensual pursuits. And in the past, I believed if I was good at sex that everyone would love me. Though it didn't bring me love, it filled me with heartache and pain.

Now, I believe that my cup is the vessel, my vessel, my womb space, my entire temple. It's me. It's the chalice in which my soul resides, and I choose how to fill my cup and what to fill it with.

I no longer expect anybody else to fill me, complete me, as I know that my chalice begins to run over by fully showing up every day for *me* with strong, consistent boundaries.

In the past, I had such expectations for everyone external to me to make me feel better, love me, and bring me joy that if I found my person, I would be whole. However, I didn't realize that the only person who can make me happy is me.

I believed that if I filled my cup with enough fun, love, and good times the light within me would grow larger.

However, what I was doing was opening an expensive bottle of wine and tipping it into a cup that had been lying in the toxic mud. I rarely drink these days, though I know that'd taste pretty rubbish. There would be grit and dirt everywhere, and I'd have just thrown away money on that very expensive wine.

Then I thought to myself, *What would happen if I emptied my cup and refilled it? How do you empty your cup and fill it again?*

The first thing is to start saying *yes* to *you* and stop doing what others want you to do. Then clean your cup, though that may take you into the void.

What is it to find yourself in the void?

Once you decide to put yourself first, and it will be a hard decision like leaving a long-term partner or another inspirational life-changing decision, you're really stepping into a new level of self-love, knowing your boundaries, and knowing yourself. And *yes*, you will ask, *Who am I?* once you've stepped into the void.

The void is a place filled with infinite possibilities, though this may feel very strange because you have been pretending that life is great for so long that you are not sure what to do with infinite possibilities.

It can be really scary, though it can be where the true adventure begins. The void is the moments when you don't know who you are anymore. You've lost the identity of who you thought you were, as it was only a persona of a person that was attempting to fit in to get external validation and love.

It takes a little time before you can look in the mirror and say, 'This is me. This is why I'm here on this earth, and this is what I love to do.'

For me, my void moment came after leaving a twenty-three-year relationship, where I totally lost myself. To be honest, I don't even know if I knew myself to begin with. I had no boundaries, I had no self-worth, and I didn't believe that I deserved better in my life.

I didn't know what I liked to do or if it was something I did to hopefully receive some love.

I was in a rush to feel better, to find myself, to be healed, and to want to love again.

Though you will need to wait a period to allow yourself to return to a neutral state of being. A period to come back to the zero point, ground level, to come back to you. And while you're returning to that ground level, life can be very uncomfortable. Since you thought that once you made that life-changing decision, all the dramas would disappear, and life would be wonderful. Although it doesn't disappear, the pain, the heartache, all of the things that culminated for you to make that decision within that moment, that perfect moment for you, they all need to be seen and heard and felt after being squirreled away in that box for so long.

It'd be so nice if all that pain and anguish disappeared with a click. Unfortunately, it doesn't.

Feeling fear in the moments when we move through pain and suffering and wade through the darkness is where we learn lessons that help us move forward. We can empty that box so we aren't carrying those burdens. We think to ourselves, *Have I made the right decision? Should I go back? What have I done?* This is for the void. The unknown seems so vast with possibilities, and you have been running on empty for so long. This is part of the process. Breathe deep and allow true faith to wash over your being.

This is about emptying the cup, your chalice, and your vessel so that you can refill it with beautiful nourishment and nourishment that you love yourself.

Yes, yes, yes, my darling, you did make that action. You made that move, with that beautiful notion of self-love, the ultimate commitment to yourself, the toughest decision you've made to this date. Just know that there is always that little bit more healing that needs to happen before we can step into the magic of the new life.

Sometimes we need to fully shut down for real change to happen so we can return to ourselves and not be able to do everything for everybody else. This is a pause in our life. This pause is the cup deep within the mud, allowing all the feelings to be seen and heard, taking full responsibility that you allowed the cup to be left in the mud, and it's up to you to clean her off and bring her back to the shelf before she is full again.

That pause may take a month or two, or it could take as long as a year. You just need to honor yourself and listen to what your body is telling you. Allow yourself the time you need to come back to *you*, back to your heart space. And your body will know when you're ready to start taking on the world again, however that might work for you. Whether it's taking on a new position and career, or a new partner, you'll know. Within your heart, you'll feel a spark. You'll feel alive again if you take those small steps or maybe even a few big ones, and you'll start to shine. You'll illuminate the beautiful purpose of your soul and bring forth your magic to the world.

Let's just take a moment here and now to see what your body is saying.

Take a moment and find a space to sit where no one will disturb you. It could be your favorite place, like a beach or a forest, or it could be on your couch. There is no right or wrong. The point here is to make time for you.

Close your eyes and take three mindful breaths.

Breathe in for the count of eight.

Breathe out for the count of eight.

Breathe in for the count of eight.

Breathe out for the count of eight.

Breathe in for the count of eight.

Breathe out for the count of eight.

I invite you now to see, sense, and imagine a beautiful golden ray of light beaming down from above, coming through the crown of your head, down through the brow or third eye point, filling your head with this golden light, down past your throat allowing you the ability to speak from truth, then bringing the light to your tender heart. You now notice that this same golden illuminated light is shining from beneath your feet, from the crystalline core of Gaia, moving its way up through your feet, through your legs, to the base of your spine. Up to the sacrum, through to your tummy and your solar plexus, and then connecting once again at your heart.

Breathe in deeply as you feel connected, safer, and held.

Now take a moment to connect with your body energetically—you may wish to place one hand over your heart and one over your womb space while doing this.

What is your body saying? Now, if your mind starts to think about anything, thank the thoughts, come back to your breath, and actually think to yourself, *Body, what are you feeling?*

You may sit for as long as you can, five minutes to start with, and then increase the time every day. The more often you do this, the deeper you will connect with your body.

Your body also may say that it needs to move, do what will bring your body the greatest amount of joy—in that space, you will find the answers and the guidance you need.

This leads me back to emptying the cup.

This is where the work begins after being held captive to others' needs and wants. It's time to look at the emotions we've held within our bodies. We need to cleanse these emotions and beliefs energetically because we may have become addicted to the *Five Fs* in our body: *Fight, Flight, Freeze, Fawn, and Flop*.

We aren't born to crave conflict in our lives, though if we conflict with someone, we can start to get our needs met. However, this is filling up the cup with toxic behaviors, potentially because of the belief systems that our subconscious is running on. The thoughts that you don't deserve to be fully loved at your soul's level. I believe this is probably the most important part of the process, especially as we're making our way through the unknown.

Our expectation of self and others is a big thing to empty from the cup. This emptying will probably take a few goes, but the more your cup is empty and then filled with deliciousness you won't need anything from anyone else. This brings me back to my first angel, Ayla Mae. I expected her to fill my life with love and joy. Now, I just see her as my mirror who brings me the greatest lessons, no expectations from each other, only unconditional love.

As a woman, I've held onto generational wounding from my matriarchal line for over eleven generations. I've done a lot of work to cleanse my cup. So how very curious that a song that keeps me grounded to my purpose is one that my grannie sang to me. My great-great-grandmother, Maude, has been with me as I move through my own personal void. As well as a curse that goes back to Italy to my Great Nonna Isabella and her daughter Rose. I named my second child Isabella Rose.

I want to send love, deep gratitude, and acknowledgment to all of the women within my line. Thank you for gracing me with all of the wonderful gifts and guiding me to find my illuminated voice.

When we transmute emotions from our body, there is generally a release that will happen, snot crying which turns to joyful tears, belching through to dry-retching or even vomiting, yawning, sneezing, coughing, breaking wind to diarrhea. Even physical appearance can change, like losing weight or looking more feminine. Though the one that I love the most is the glow that someone gets after they have shed the weight of energies that have been weighing them down. For me, that's the luminescent glow of your soul within your body, and as you vibrate at a higher vibration, you can hold your glow for longer.

Feeling your *yes* within your body can be painful sometimes, but it can be the most magical journey you can take yourself on.

It's about finally standing with yourself on a pedestal and congratulating yourself for choosing the most important person in your world, *you*. It's about illuminating brighter and brighter as the big, fluffy heart you are and knowing that if you align with your big, beautiful heart, the right people will come into your life, and you no longer have to fit within anyone's box.

I now take myself to the beach weekly, rain, hail, or shine. This gives me the space to go through a cup-emptying process so that when I'm filling my cup, it's filled with the knowing that I'm my own infinite love connection.

It's finally having the courage to connect deeply to my womb and to

Conscious Revolution

Goddess Gaia, spread love from my heart, open to my galactic advisers, and start singing those words to the hymn that rolls through my being, repeating in round robin style, *Running Over, Running Over.*

I now know that when I illuminate rainbows from my being, I'm a beacon to guide others toward remembering that they are their own infinite love connection. That when you choose to love yourself completely, there is a way through the pain and the void. When you accept that the vast space is the perfect birthing place for creation, a place where we can all illuminate our hearts across the realm, ensuring that everyone has a cup that is running over with *love*.

A poem by Samantha-Jayne Love—inspired by the hymn *Running Over.*

My Chalice is Running Over
Breathe in, my dear, and feel all that there is to feel
Breathe out all of the pain and suffering
You are safe and secure here, my dear
Come home to me no need to persevere

Breathe in, my dear, this life isn't meant to be filled with pain
Breathe out, and call in all of the queens who reign
Remember your chalice. Allow your tears to flow like streams
See your cup you've filled her with the most amazing dreams

You deserve for your chalice to run over
You deserve all of the love a thousand times over
Wishes can come true. Stars align for you
'Cos you deserve for your chalice to run over

About Samantha-Jayne

Hello, beautiful beings,

My name is Samantha-Jayne Love. I am an illuminated love expert and international self-empowerment, love, and soul facilitator who works with the conscious, unconscious, spirit, mind, and energy bodies for your being. What a wild ride it's been to get to the place where I am.

Ever since I was a little girl, I wanted to be a mum and have a baby because I wanted to love and be loved so deeply. I craved love and attention from everyone external to myself and found that I'd get some of the void filled by performing, so I sang, danced, and acted, which I believed fulfilled me.

From sixteen, I was unconsciously attempting to become pregnant. Then when I was eighteen, I fell in love with the young man I believed to be the one. We were engaged, and I hoped each cycle would be the one that would bring me the joy of becoming a mother.

Conscious Revolution

Unfortunately, as we grew, we grew apart. Then at twenty-three I was heartbroken and alone, which created a vortex of very destructive behaviors. This was when I met my ex-husband, and from this toxic place, I fell in love and forgot about myself, though I still knew I longed for a baby to love and hold.

Along this journey, I was able to get pregnant. Unfortunately, the little souls would hitch a ride and then leave my body. I've had twenty-five pregnancies, though I only have two beautiful little angels that call me Mumma.

When the first girl was born, I was filled with joy, love, and wonder though it was clouded with sadness, fear, and anxiety as I believed my dream would get taken away from all the other things I loved. Welcome postnatal depression, which I attempted to cover up from the outside because I wanted everyone to see what a brilliant life I had.

I'd act like I had a perfect life talking the talk, and I would learn new skills and awaken my soul because if I did enough work on myself, everything would be okay.

So, this powerhouse studied and became the embodiment of the divine feminine. With my skills in Fembodiment Method (level two) facilitator, womb magic, sexual sovereignty, sacred starlight temple guide, self-empowerment coach, International Freedom Protocol master practitioner, counsellor, life coaching, hypnosis, sacred circle facilitator, there are many, many more, my toolbox is full, I was taken on a journey of self-discovery, which I get to guide others on now.

I spent twenty-three years putting everyone else before me then I decided to start walking my walk and separated from my husband in 2022, the hardest and most freeing thing I have ever done.

For the past twenty-five years, I've been working with people and helping them go on a journey toward mental and spiritual wellness. I love working with my spiritual team to awaken your body, realign, and fill your chalice with illuminated love. I want to help you regain an appreciation

Samantha-Jayne Love

for the lessons learned while in the uneasiness of life, all with agency and consent, and transcend into the transformed you. I want to show you what it's like to illuminate and know that you deserve all that your heart desires.

Find Samantha-Jayne Love at:
Website: samanthajayne.love
Facebook: facebook.com/samanthajayne.love
Instagram: instagram.com/samanthajayne_love
YouTube: youtube.com/c/LOVETALKwithSamanthaJayneLove

Find Infinite Love Connection at:
Website: infiniteloveconnection.com
Facebook: facebook.com/infiniteloveconnection
Instagram: instagram.com/infiniteloveconnection
YouTube: youtube.com/c/InfiniteLoveConnection

Mitzi Rae

CHILDREN AT HEART

As a child, I wondered why we were here and felt there was more to life than what seemed to be present. Such curiosity has led me to experiences where I've discovered so much more than we have ever been taught in traditional educational institutions.

As a holistic practitioner, I'm intrigued and excited about possibilities. Many people live with pain and illness daily and long to expand in their current being (heart, mind, spirit, consciousness). It's my goal to connect people to their bodies, help them heal, and know their own power. I believe with my whole heart and soul in healing and our body's ability and innate wisdom to heal. In each individual's capacity, there is magnificence to be felt and seen when one can discover expansion beyond their perceived limitations and embrace their uniqueness.

I appreciate people. I see to a great depth, the beauty in them. People who I connect with from afar when I hear their stories, what they have done in this life, challenges they face. To those who I know but may not know personally so well, and my amazing peeps who I am eternally grateful for knowing, having in my life, and sharing this journey with.

~ If only you could see you the way I see you. ~

Spiritual awakening is not all fluffy love and light and rainbows. It is confronting and can be jarring and intense. When we awaken to the systems that have taught us how to be and live, we see beyond the illusion and conditioning. We can free ourselves from these systems to be in our own flow and uniqueness. When we go inward for answers and connect with like-minded and like-hearted people, we see our own truth at heart. We become curious about what is possible. We see the gaps in what has been taught to us, in what has pre-filled our minds and manipulated our beliefs. We connect to the suffering of people in this world. Instead of feeling powerless, we empower ourselves by focusing on what we can do for ourselves and our communities, trusting that this will ripple out to the collective. We become our own teachers and discover our own wisdom within. Our bodies are amazing vessels with which we interact with our physical world and with which we can create from and into our physical reality.

In my late teens, I read the book *How to Make ESP Work for You* by Harold Sherman (1964), which includes Sherman's experiences from the 1920s onwards. It was interesting to see people's reactions when I took the book to work one day, 'Oooh ESP,' like it was something very weird. What I took from the book was that it wasn't weird to me; it was logical and explained practical ways to use extrasensory abilities in our everyday lives.

Reading this book gave me the first insight into the power we have in healing our own bodies. I profoundly remember the chapter on healing, where Sherman had gangrene in his foot, and as painful and awful as it was, he healed himself by visualizing his foot as being perfectly healthy. He also enlisted others to hold the same intention and visualization to assist with his healing. There is so much other great stuff in the book too, including telepathy, premonitions, his own experiments, and more. Now reflecting on Sherman's insights and teachings, I can see that this is all possible through the generation and transference of energy. With pure intention, anything is possible.

Along my own journey of processing my own stuff, self-reflection, and self-healing, I've discovered the process of healing can be super intense but always so worth it. In doing so, I've let go of strong opinions and limiting beliefs. Instead, in the moment of reaction, I can see more from an observer's perspective, which gives space to look beyond the reaction or what could be happening for someone or myself. I then have a choice in how *I* will be about it.

Healing can be seen as a painful process. I feel that it's not really healing that carries the pain. It's what's been too hard to deal with, what has made us unsafe, or has gone unacknowledged for a long time. Acknowledging these life events and emotions is part of the healing process. Healing is the part that allows us to see what is and what is beyond—feeling lightness, no longer carrying a burden that infiltrated so intricately the psyche, and cellular memory and function. The clarity that comes when the veils are lifted, limiting beliefs are shed, and new strengths emerge.

Will we ever truly be healed? I believe so, in terms of what's held in our bodies, mind, and spirit from this journey and past journeys. We may get to that final layer of that one event, or of many events, and transform it. However, you will experience new life events, and it doesn't mean we won't need to continue caring for ourselves and healing, nor that we forget all we have been through. We develop the tools to deal in new ways as our spirit evolves, where we'll see the difference in how things once affected us, we see new perspectives, and we have conscious choices. We hold new intentions that aren't fear-based but come from love and respect. When you arrive at such consciousness, you can celebrate how miraculous you *really* are. There will always be new challenges to face in life. Embrace them and know that you do your best with what you know at any given moment. Discover what works for you in seeking support in healing, connect with and embrace your soul family, and know that you're not alone and that what you feel and experience is all valid.

Some people are reluctant to change, whether conscious of it or not. I get the resistance. It may seem that evolving in consciousness is preceded by a *conscious mess!* My experience has been that feeling shock, stress, and a myriad of emotions is part of the journey. Navigating through this has ultimately led me to new perspectives. In a broader sense, inner work can heal intergenerational trauma. It's in our actions, for example, how we care for our children or extend our understanding and kindness to our brothers and sisters who just need to be heard and seen for who they really are and not consent to control and manipulation.

Through deep grief, I've been able to process. Where I once was caught up so deep in it, I couldn't see how it was possible to *let go*. I have an identical twin sister, Sumiko. We were preemie babies. I was firstborn, and my sister was born sixteen minutes after. I reflect and think of how difficult it was for Mum not to be able to take us home, as we had to stay in an incubator crib for six weeks. Mum would come every day to see us and feed us. We were never apart except for one occasion that I recall when my sister stayed with an aunt for a night.

Between two and four years old, we went to live in Japan with the man my mother married. My memories of him were that he was volatile and abusive. We moved back to Perth with Mum. I was very shy, and as we went to several different primary schools in Perth and the South-West before moving to Port Hedland, I felt I needed my sister close. I guess it was some anxiety at the notion of a new environment and people we didn't know, even though I didn't know what anxiety was until my adult life. In reality, Sumi probably felt the same way but put on a brave face for me.

My sister was very creative and artistic, and even though I may have achieved slightly higher grades at school, she was more mature and got things I didn't get. She was way cooler than me as we went into what is now called the 'pre-teen' years. Sumi passed during the Christmas holidays after our thirteenth birthday from a severe asthma attack.

That night we were staying with a family friend. Sumi had had a headache earlier. My mum and her partner at the time relayed advice to this lady, who was like an aunt to us, on how to give mouth-to-mouth resuscitation via the phone. I was with my sister. She couldn't breathe, and just before she collapsed, her last words to me were, 'I don't want to die.' To which I replied, 'You're not going to die.'

I didn't think she would. I hadn't thought of the seriousness of her illness, even though she'd been hospitalized previously for asthma attacks. She said something else I couldn't make out, her last breaths and voice dwindling. The ambulance took forever to arrive. I was upset by this point and went outside. 'Hurry up!'

I don't remember the ambulance officers, what they did. But they took my sister. I remember sitting with our family friend. I think she tried to help me by asking if I wanted a cup of tea or if I wanted to play cards, though I was unsure exactly what. I woke the next morning to Mum and her partner coming into the room. 'Sumi didn't make it.' I didn't understand. It would take me well into my adult life to understand.

The outside world seemed so surreal in the days following. I remember being at a shopping center and thinking, *How can people just go on about their lives?* The funeral was a blur, but I remember my great-uncle saying, 'Just let those tears fall.' But I was numb. I appreciate those words and realize I have said the same to others in support in recent years. My great-uncle was one of only two decent males I knew growing up, both of whom I wish I'd gotten to know better and spent more time with as a child. Mum chose the song *Imagine* by John Lennon to play at Sumi's funeral. We had a boat service out at sea from our northern coastal hometown, where Mum placed her ashes into the ocean.

I would cry a lot. When on my own. I heard there were rumors going around school about how she died that weren't true. I was afraid of the supernatural element. Somewhat ironic as it intrigued me so, and Sumi loved to read ghost stories! At some point, I must have chosen to try to block out the pain. In doing so I blocked her out.

Years later, I became consciously aware that I was living like it was my fault. I didn't save her. Shortly after she passed, we learned about first aid, resuscitation, and CPR at school. I felt that we should have been taught earlier. Why didn't I know this? I should have known.

Around nineteen, I did a three-day first aid course during my electrical apprenticeship. I masked the discomfort I felt over the duration of the course. I spoke to the instructor, who advised when I asked about asthma that there would still be part of the airway open, but whether this was the case for my sister remains unknown. This only confirmed that I should have done more to help her.

I have done first aid courses since. I did one last year, a requirement of attending placements for my university degree studying to be an occupational therapist. I find the instructors to be amazing people. Also, asthma is a part of the course. It was good to learn how spacers are now used for people with asthma, making the Ventolin inhalers more effective. Recently my aunt shared that Sumi was very self-conscious about using her Ventolin inhaler in front of people.

This gave me more insight into how Sumi felt about her illness.

I have carried the blame for my sister's death, living with this without conscious awareness. It was just how it was. There was also guilt that I got to live when she didn't. The guilt for blocking her out when I just didn't know how to deal. There was emptiness accompanied by the pain of loss and grief. So deep that I have had profound moments of realization, in healing, concerning losing my twin sister from this plane of existence.

How to know my own identity when it was enmeshed with another who wasn't here? The intricate layers surfaced one after another, yet with what seemed like lifetimes in-between. I have come to accept what I knew and didn't know at the time. The breakdowns and breakthroughs were initially very physical, like migraines and vomiting. In later years, more layers surfaced as I continued following my curiosity and wanting to better myself and my life situations. Processing grief was not always so physical, very emotional. Still, some pain was felt in my body.

Through processing and acknowledging my feelings and through various healings, such as breath work, sound healing, plant medicine, self-healing, and intuition, I gained an expanded understanding. I understood that she was needed elsewhere. I reflected on and honored her and who she was here on earth and acknowledged that my feelings were valid.

My apology was held deep in my throat, a physical block I felt when I held her in front of me in a guided meditation to feel her love and send my love. 'I'm sorry, I'm sorry, I'm sorry.' She did not judge. That was mine. I wanted to hold her in love, as I knew she had been holding me. Realizing that I could not feel her love previously was my own doing.

Intertwined on my journey of self-love, this was a deep layer. To acknowledge for myself what I say so open-heartedly and often to others, 'Have compassion for yourself.' Now I can think of Sumi without the intense pain and sadness. I still miss her dearly. And I know she isn't far. She has been with me all along, and I am with her, even when I wasn't consciously aware of this. I am so grateful that we got to come into this life together and share all that we have shared.

I reflect on all of my experiences; they have helped me be even more empathetic in relating to people and what they go through. In this occurrence, I acknowledge it is no coincidence that I have seen clients who have lost their twin. I appreciate these connections.

The past few years, in particular, have seen me through trials and tribulations. I've endured challenges that have been the catalyst for *big* changes in my life. Due to my personal choices, I have not yet been able to complete my occupational therapy degree (with one unit to complete), and I was stood down from my workplace of seventeen years. None of the houndings from every external angle and discrimination that I and many others faced could sway me from my resounding 'no' embedded deep within. Founded by the heartbreak I felt, having seen what was happening to people in other countries long before this series of events came to Australia. I understand there was a lot of fear driving this. I hold compassion for all no matter their views or beliefs on this particular leg of the journey. Many have suffered on all sides, and I don't discount all that I've witnessed playing out. But we've lost sight that sides are an illusion.

As a customer, I went into the optical retail store I worked in a few months ago, not having been there for several months since I was no longer welcome. A friend and work colleague commented, 'No work, no stress.' As I later reflected, I found it incredible and interesting that this perception was so far from the reality of what I've been through. I, along with so many people, were faced with the prospect of how I was going to manage to keep my home, provide for my daughter, look after my dog, pay bills, and have enough food. We were locked out of job opportunities. Fear was definitely one of the many emotions I faced. There was an apparent void in being heard. Such is the systemic reach. I became mindful of where to focus my energy and where not to. I had to manage things differently, manage my finances differently, and trust that no matter what, I could maintain the essentials.

I had signed up for the Spinal Flow Technique program and put studying the course on hold while finishing my degree. However, the timing was perfect as the spinal flow immersion training that I'd registered for coincided. It was so powerful and amazing! I already wanted to start my own business doing healing work, having completed reiki level two previously, and I loved the philosophy and science of Spinal Flow. I've worked hard to start my own business, learning along the way.

At the first big birthday celebration I'd been to since 2020, a strange feeling came over me. *I should be enjoying this party,* realizing all I'd been holding within was coming to the surface. It took some work to process through and realize that I didn't have to be on alert or need to watch my back here. Perhaps this was the trigger for my inquiry into the feeling of needing to be *careful*. It became apparent how ingrained this had become into elements of my being from various sources of personal experiences. I am grateful for this insight.

The hardest part throughout the past two years, in particular, is having family members who have been ill. The crises, emergency room visits, and calling ambulances for my loved ones. The caring for and sheer moments of high stress and worry. The fear of loss. The *what do I do?* The going through the motions. The hoping and praying. The heartbreak. Nothing like watching someone you love suffering and feeling like there's nothing you can do to help them. The just keep going—the coming back to TRUST.

Looking back on my work and study situation, it's all been perfect. It was the push for me onto the path where I needed to be. I see how the focus on medical diagnosis and prognosis can be limiting for people. Alongside this, I've learned how illness and disease manifest in the body. I've learned so much about how amazing our bodies are and how powerful we really are.

It's an absolute honor and a pleasure to connect with and work with people. I love what I do. I will keep working to grow my practice and make a difference for people, myself, and my daughter. I have an amazing soul tribe that I'm so grateful for, and I've found that I'm meeting more amazing souls. Finding and connecting with my soul sisters has been a beautiful blessing, the ones who get you, and you get them, no matter how quirky or woo-woo. And the energy output when we come together is phenomenal! The deeper connection to self, honoring, and knowing thyself.

I have come to realize that I don't have 'guides' as such, that I perceive as others do, although I do feel support. It's been just me and my heart leading me. In times of indecisiveness or seeking answers, this has become apparent. And maybe, those who have guidance from other beings are tuning into the wisdom of other aspects of themselves. This leads me to ponder the true meaning of the *universe*. As well as the knowledge that we are creator beings, we create our reality, such is the power of our thoughts and beliefs, including limiting beliefs about ourselves, that vibrationally transmit and interact with our ionosphere and beyond. As such, what comes to us reflects an aspect of what is within us. I do believe this with one exception, which is abuse, and abuse of one's power over another to attempt to take what is not theirs—the innocence of another.

What saddens me the most in this life is how people treat each other and animals. Having witnessed violence as a young child and not having a decent male role model (I could tell more, but that would be a whole other book). I am eternally grateful that Mum kept us away from harm as much as possible, breaking cycles of abuse from her generation and the generations before. Even so, there were incidences of predatory agendas. Sadly, most people have at least one story.

I believe we must go through hardship in order to grow. However, I also believe there is interference, causing stress and suffering to the greater extent that I see in our world, coupled with the conditioning to look outside ourselves for how we ought to live, hindering self-actualization. When all around you makes no sense, come back to your heart. For each individual, perception varies, and this perception informs one's truth. It is a blessing to realize you get to choose how you are going to be and what your reality will be. It's an inside job.

I have learned that unconditional love is more about yourself, recognizing attachments to outcomes, where defenses come from, ways of being, and responding. You cannot control what others do or what happens in life. You can influence. Though your own actions towards your own life and living from guidance from within are the best ways to create the changes you want to see for yourself, your loved ones, and for the greater good.

I acknowledge the purpose of all of my experiences. My evolution so far has taught me to stand up for myself. I no longer relinquish my power to another, and I do not consent to interference. I do not consent to being controlled, held, or doing things against my will. I may still worry at times, and I can still hold compassion for others, but I no longer live from fear. I also own my own stuff and how my ways of being have impacted others. I apologize, do my best to make amends, try not to beat myself up about it, and learn from it. I am constantly challenging my belief systems and observing. I see in a positive light, for equally, yet exponentially, there has been joy and happiness, even if for seemingly fleeting moments.

When you unravel the layers of distortion, you are in your truth, your pure essence. Discover that you have within all the love that is needed, that you may have felt like you missed out on, or that you may have pushed for in relationships onto the other people to give. In this discovery, there is a choice to shift from entitlement to empowerment, releasing attachment to outcomes. While this process may not feel as easy as it sounds, the result is feeling a new sense of freedom.

You can create new neural pathways and alter your vibrational frequency, for example, as I have done through practice, transforming negative self-talk (insults, profanity, name-calling) to words of support, love, and encouragement.

Even so, those more covert layers of denigration lingered to put their two cents in at times. I acknowledged and thanked these psychological mechanisms for their duty, offered compassion and reassurance, and chose differently. When these wounds heal, space is created for the new to come in. We can regain trust in ourselves and others and take risks in the face of fear, for we know what we have endured and processed, and we know we are all stronger for it. The mind tells us what we can't withstand. The heart knows it can withstand anything. The heart is here to experience all, full spectrum.

Perhaps we knew at the soul level before coming to earth what we were in for. I do believe that, at this time, there is the greatest chance to help humanity, break cycles, and heal our trauma so we can stop passing it to our children and the following generations. We can ensure to the best of our ability that our children won't come to harm by another with ill intent. Anxiety can come from feeling unsafe in past situations. If one can work through to a place of safety within, however that works for each individual, while not forgoing living a fulfilled life, that would be a great goal to work towards. Of course, it's more easily said than done. Healing modalities, for example, in a gentle way, can assist in this, and I've seen it in my clients who can feel calmer, lighter and sleep better, which positively impacts their daily lives. It's also important to note that anxiety can be a response in the body that something isn't right for us and to discern when this is the case and honor it for ourselves.

MOVING FROM FEAR TO LOVE

I acknowledge fear as an important function. Fear has many layers and masks of alternate emotions and drives behaviors that masquerade as something other than the fear. Truly that is what is at the root, and then there is what is behind the fear.

The beauty is that love also has many layers. Infinite, I imagine!

Share your heart but don't give your heart away. You get the say in who you are. Your heart is huge, and it's yours. It's for YOU.

In ascension, we evolve in consciousness. Earth is also ascending in her frequency of vibration, and our bodies are vibrating at a different frequency from what we ever have before. Our bodies are recalibrating. As we traverse and navigate the spiral of evolution, a kaleidoscope of circumstantial and emotional terrain, releasing and growing, we create a new vibrational frequency, and the universe or source and earth respond.

Ascension symptoms?

You are free to take what resonates from what is being shared in the spiritual community about ascension symptoms. There is a lot of great content by amazing people offering their support. However, I recommend being discerning and listening to you and your body above all.

Conscious Revolution

Clearing what's held in the body can make us more sensitive to energy, be more empathic, and have more awareness of our own sensitivity, emotionally, physically, and spiritually. Caring for our own needs and teaching our children to care for themselves are important. How we care for ourselves is an ongoing process into adulthood for us to be mindful of. As we shift, we become more aware of how we need to care for ourselves and our energy.

SELF-CARE AND SELF-LOVE

Discern what is and isn't yours to take on. Nurture you and do what brings you comfort, even if it means days in bed, because sometimes you might just need this. Do anything that brings a sense of peace and freedom. Ground yourself often in nature.

Have compassion for yourself. A reminder is needed now and again because it's so easy to say to other people and become complacent for ourselves. See the bigger picture, all-encompassing, from the soul level, especially in those heart-wrenching moments.

Self-love sounds simple and maybe cliché. It's difficult to fully understand self-love until you have experience. It's a dynamic process, with generally much resistance in the beginning.

Accept all parts of yourself, what you do, how you feel without judgment, seeing what is, is. Acknowledge your inner child saying, *Hear me,* and embrace them in support. The more love we feel for ourselves, the more we honor our boundaries. The more love we can receive, means we have an expanded level of love and compassion for those around us.

See children for who they are—'resilience', I believe, comes from connection, the knowledge they are heard and supported. Treat yourself the same way, seek support and be your own cheerleader when you need to. To nurture and give the physical body attention, nutrition, exercise, rest, affection, sunlight, water, and listening to what it wants to tell us; in this way, we are telling the body, *I love you,* and we can thrive.

As much as there is work, enjoying ourselves is important. Keep optimism, positivity, and curiosity. What lights you up and brings you joy? Make time to do the things that you love to do that you haven't done in a long time. Surround yourself with people who support your values, work, goals, and dreams, whom you feel energized around, whom you can be yourself around, whom you can relax and have fun with.

Acknowledge all that you have achieved—the wisdom you've discovered. There is so much to acknowledge, to be celebrated about you!

COUNT YOUR BLESSINGS

Give gratitude to our great Mother Earth, who holds and nurtures us. I'm grateful to have a home that provides shelter and running water. I thank water; water cleanses, hydrates, warms, or cools down. When I wash veggies, I hold intention with the running water to neutralize what isn't good for us and to draw the nutrients in its purity from the food for my family. I thank the food beings. I thank Mother Earth for providing. I thank the people who have worked to grow and transport the food. I thank the sun, air, and wind for drying my clothes, for the warmth, the energy, and the breezes that bring wisdom and comfort.

I'm grateful for the amazing people in my life. A daughter who amazes me every day, my greatest teacher, seer of truth, who sees bullcrap and calls it out. She has the hugest heart and also knows what she won't put up with. Angel of pure light. Gratitude to my twelve-year-old dog, who taught me more about unconditional love. I am grateful for my mums, my family, and chosen family. The strong women in my family are my heroes.

BE JOYFUL

True adulting is really just becoming more childlike.

Rediscover the wonderful qualities that a child emanates. Be in the moment and present with what is around us. Be joyful and in a state of play. Connect with the magic and fun of imagination, the sense of adventure, enthusiasm, and excitement in every game you play.

Immerse in humor and laughter. What gives you a sense of wonder? What brings you delight?

LETTING GO OF THE LIFE YOU PLANNED

Those tower moments are blessings, an opportunity to rewrite the script of your life, and alter the performance to direct your path with heart-led intention. We are generators and receivers of energy. We are creators of our own freedom. When you know your true self, the universe (uni = you) will provide. The manifestation tends to happen in ways you might not expect and can feel even better than you first imagined. There will be so many distractions, tempting offers, and interesting things to learn and explore. New pathways will appear that are heart-aligned.

You get to discern and choose. You get to choose what you will engage with, what your truth is, and what you want to create, perhaps something that has never been done before.

When you can go to the depths and heights that allow you to create from your heart, mind, spirit, and being in totality, you get to create and choose the meaning of your life.

What is it that you want to create in this world?

Feeling in your body and being, what are your resounding noes and resounding yeses? What is your unique expression?

UNBRIDLE YOUR MAGIC, WRITE YOUR OWN LEGEND

Consider diversity and the greater ecosystem of nature. Earth heals herself. Our Indigenous peoples' culture embedded this integral, sacred connection and continue to hold the wisdom and knowledge. Healing happens when one goes back to country. We are an expression of our great Mother Earth, just as we are of source itself.

We are the flowers of life—opening up. The more we do this, the more those around us do the same. And we comprehend we are intricately connected, as flowers are, in the shared parenting plants, the root systems, the soil.

We are the warriors of the heart.

About Mitzi

I have strong family values, and I am a proud mum of my amazing teenage daughter. My career history consists of various types of work, including an electrical apprenticeship; engaging with people as an optical dispenser (seventeen years), and various customer service roles prior; supporting women in refuge; studying occupational therapy and research; and volunteering for environmental groups and other causes. I am now working as a holistic practitioner, helping people with physical and emotional healing. I am also working towards my dream of working with our youth, in providing a space that they can feel heard and supported, and be empowered to live fulfilling lives, be their unique selves, and bring their magic to our world.

I am fascinated by diversity in nature, I value inclusivity, and I tend to be attracted to what is 'different' or 'new', that which I find intriguing, and what I resonate with. Along with life changes and experiences, through my community connections, I was drawn to learn about energy and holistic healing; a profound journey that has enhanced my beliefs about what is possible. My compassion for people, and my focus on health and well-being, has led me to actively practice reiki and the Spinal Flow Technique.

I carry a long-held dream of holistic healing (and there are so many wonderful modalities) and the medical industry coming together and complimenting one another, so that people can have choice, and the appropriate person-centered care that has the best outcomes for them. I have seen that this is slowly starting to take place. I love how Spinal Flow combines science and spirituality. I have a keen interest in neuroscience and neuroplasticity, often exploring the energetic component—the integration of energy within our nervous system and our whole bodies. I have observed where stress is held in our bodies, in my clients, and in my own personal experiences, and how with energetic healing, the body is facilitated to shift from a state of excessive stress to deep relaxation. Our bodies can then be receptive to healing what has been causing pain, illness, and/or what has been preventing people from living life in the way that their hearts desire. I am excited about what is possible for people, passionate about connecting people with their bodies, to rediscover their innate power and wisdom, in healing, freedom, and in what brings them joy.

Find me at:
Facebook: facebook.com/RadicalHeartExpansion
Email: radicalheartexpansion@gmail.com

Jenny Arnold

I KNOW WHICH WAY I'M GOING

Some might say a spiritual awakening occurs naturally over a long time, but it mostly occurs following a significant event or tragedy in one's life. Mine was certainly the latter. Heartbreaking events in 2018 definitely woke me up with an almighty shake of the ground, and my world changed forever. Not only was I crushed beyond belief and heartbroken, but terrified for my life. This was to be my conscious revolution.

In April 2018, I had been monitoring a lump in my right breast. A mammogram, ultrasounds, biopsies, and then a lumpectomy of apparently an abnormal cyst followed. Unfortunately, this happened on May 14, and I had to wait for the results while I recovered. Then, on May 19, I had the worst phone call ever.

When you know a loved family member is sick and elderly, you're kind of waiting but are never prepared for that phone call, my gorgeous grandad passed over following months of prostate cancer and deteriorating health, and I was devastated. I spent so much of my childhood with him most weekends and every holiday, following him around everywhere he went. I was called his little shadow. He was the significant male figure in my life as my father wasn't around. With all this going on, I felt so cut off from the rest of the family. I was in Australia, my family was in the UK, and I felt so alone.

May 29 is another date etched into my brain. Test results revealed the lump removed was ductal carcinoma in situ (DCIS). I remember that day so clearly. My nineteen-year-old son sat waiting for me in the waiting room, and all I could think about was how I could tell him I had breast cancer. I couldn't let it sink in. The doctor said I could have another operation to make a clearance, as the cancer was bigger than they expected, then six weeks of radiation, or I could have a mastectomy.

I was in a blur, and my mind was spinning, but he gave me time to think and digest. How could I comprehend what was happening to me? I was given so many leaflets and printouts to read. It was like that scene in a movie where the nurse speaks to you, but you've zoned out. You can't hear a word they're saying. You're just numb and in shock. So, I just nodded my head and left with hands full of leaflets and a pretty pink folder about cancer. I wasn't only grieving for my grandad and trying to study, but now I had to focus on this. I went on autopilot, doing as much research as possible.

We had a family meeting, and the kids were braver than I felt. I decided it had to be a mastectomy. My instinct was strong that this was the best decision for me, not just one side but both breasts. I just didn't want the worry that it would return, and the instincts I felt were strong enough to guide me. There were five women that same week diagnosed with DCIS. I had to go to counseling to make sure I was making the right decision for a double mastectomy, and I ended up discussing past traumas in my life. She helped me see this was my time to make the right choices for me, not anyone else. This was my journey to go through.

Conscious Revolution

On September 10, 2018, I was going in for the biggest surgery of my life. A double mastectomy with DIEP reconstruction and microsurgery meant ten hours of surgery. Afterward, I lay in a heated box, a temperature-controlled room, with four drains attached to me, an ultrasound on my new breasts every fifteen minutes for twenty-four hours, checking for any rejections, and my stomach wrapped from the abdominoplasty. During recovery, I felt like I was hit by a train. I was numb emotionally and in a state of disbelief. I stayed cheerful, but that was on the outside. Inside, I was crumbling. I've always been good at that.

My instincts served me well. The results came in, and they found that my right breast had an even larger area of DCIS, which they hadn't found previously. The thought of what might have been if I hadn't had a mastectomy was too scary to comprehend, proof to trust my gut no matter what. I had no regrets, even though the recovery was a hugely painful challenge.

The thought processes following these events are indescribable. The feeling that the word *cancer* brings to you is that you face the thought of death. This is such a powerful realization that only another cancer-diagnosed person can understand. I still can't put it into words as I write this chapter. All I knew was that I wanted to embrace my life from this point forward, even if that completely changed the whole world around me.

As the weeks, months, and years passed, I found that the small stuff didn't matter to me anymore. Negativity and complaining about insignificant things didn't make sense. I couldn't stand being around it. I wanted to run away and find peace and serenity somewhere, and I started to feel a strong pull to be on my own. But I stayed because I'd been through a traumatic time and couldn't make any big decisions. I didn't realize what was happening at the time as I was too emotional, traumatized, and afraid, trying to get my head around what had just happened. This would be a long journey. I felt so lost.

I found my grandad was around me a lot during these traumatic times. He was there to comfort me and guide me. I received many spiritual healings from close friends over those few years. We discovered this cancer was likely connected to my mother's line and the trauma I experienced in my past. It can ancestrally carry over, manifesting into the physical form as it lies in all our cells and DNA.

During this time of healing, I took part in ancestral healing ceremonies, which included healing by flames, herbs, and sage smoke from Native Americans and galactic beings. My mind was opening. I discovered that the more trauma in childhood experienced, the more spiritually advanced we can become. This helped me focus more clearly and strongly on what I needed to do. I began work on cutting the ethereal cords from parental ties so I could heal my childhood. I knew I had to do what I could to remove it from my life.

I prioritized myself over everything else. Whatever wasn't meant to be in my life, I believed the universe would show me the way, even if that caused relationship breakdowns. I gave it so many chances, but it was time for me to put myself first, which I hadn't ever done before. My feelings were always controlled by others. I was always told I was too sensitive, which made me keep my feelings inside, and they built up over the years. But it was now time to speak my truth. I was being given signs everywhere.

I found new strength and empowerment inside that I'd not felt before. I learned fast that situations or people I was not meant to keep in my life had to be released. It became clear that the universe was helping me declutter my world, which was so scary.

I worked as a midwife then. It was originally my ultimate dream career, helping women in the most vulnerable time of their lives, helping them bring new life into the world. How amazingly beautiful is that? I loved the women I cared for, but the medical system started to drain me more and more. I felt so strongly in my gut that this career wasn't meant for me any longer, but living in the third-dimensional matrix, you're focused on paying bills and mortgages. And you can't see past it. So, I stayed being a midwife and got more and more frustrated. I knew what I wanted, which is what I ultimately always dreamt of, but the realization came that I never actually felt I fit in anywhere up to this point in my life. I was always searching for something else.

As a child, I saw and felt things I couldn't explain. I lived in my own imagination constantly, creating small worlds in my mind to keep myself company and help me escape my reality of neglect and abuse. I seemed to wander wherever I wanted, but we did as kids in those days. At the local pond, I found friends in the fairies, tadpoles, and creatures in nature. It was normal for me to see witches flying broomsticks in the sky on Halloween, see Jack Frost jumping across the rooftops, and hear Santa's bells on his sleigh every Christmas until I reached a certain age, I guess. I always believed that other magical beings lived in other places around us.

I got into drugs as a teenager, nothing crazy, just social partying. Then I was introduced to the rave scene. It took me to different dimensions, escaping reality. The people I met became a family, the family we all felt missing from our childhoods. The drugs helped us escape, and we all felt the love. We all had our issues to hide from. I danced and danced every weekend, free of trauma, my happy place, in my own little world again. I felt so free.

Over the years, my consciousness gave me snippets of my psychic gift, connections to family and friends when they passed over, and premonitions of earthquakes and natural disasters worldwide. Didn't everyone get this?

I started my spiritual journey in my early twenties. I met a lovely lady teaching psychic development at my local college. I joined in, not knowing what would happen and where it would take me. This is where I had my first experience with meditation. I met my first spirit guides, and we tried different psychic tools such as psychometry, third eye, and intuition exercises.

She saw something in me and was the first person to explain what this was. She felt I was a natural psychic medium. I didn't understand what that meant at the time, but she helped me connect to spirits in the classroom and gave everyone some needed messages which blew my mind. How was this so easy for me? It scared me initially. My teacher introduced me to reiki. The strong connection to source energy blew my mind daily. I achieved my reiki master level within two years. Reiki aided me in my own healing journey and vibrations, and I saw so much more as the years passed. I was happy to connect via Reiki treatments. I felt safe in that space.

Life then got busy over the next twenty years. I had two beautiful children. I felt my connections to the source fade in and out because I couldn't get in alignment. This was caused by negativity in relationships, and I kept reliving childhood traumas. I knew these needed healing first, but I had no idea where to start. It constantly simmered under the surface. As a family, we moved to Western Australia in 2013 and made it our home. We built a house, got two dogs, and lived as a family unit, but not by any means was it perfect.

In 2020, COVID-19 arrived in Australia. Vaccination mandates rolled in, and I chose not to be vaccinated to protect my health following breast cancer. I was terrified of putting any of those chemicals into my body. I shouldn't have to justify my decision. It just never seemed right to me. The alarm bells rang, and my spirit guides said no, so I listened. Shortly after, I lost my job as a midwife due to the mandates. I had a few months of real money stress. I was applying for any job during this time, thinking I was meant to start a new career. I didn't know what, I just knew I needed any job.

I focused on what I'd trained in and used the skills and experience I already had and with the funds I could to start a small business. I decided to start a market stall selling crystals. I did three or four weekly markets and loved every minute of it. Every week the universe provided me with enough money, the same as the wages I used to get doing midwifery. I realized I didn't need a job working for someone else because I was already living my dream. Obviously, this was what I was meant to do.

Back to the present day, I now realize a spiritual awakening isn't meant to be comfortable. I've separated from a long-term partner, sold the house we built eight years ago, and had more breast reconstruction surgery while starting a small business and trying to live more positively. This has been the hardest time for myself and my children, but we made it through. I met some lovely new friends along the way who have all been on their own spiritual journeys. Our energies have become so connected in a short space of time. We go to meditation groups together, which are so powerful from all the energy we create.

Our journeys have intertwined, and our spiritual group is expanding every week. I've joined a psychic development group to build my confidence in mediumship. My connection to the spirit is happening so much easier, and it blows my mind. I have found the group to be very supportive of each other, and I would definitely recommend a psychic group or circle for anyone's development.

I've moved into my own home, a space to create my *own* world, and I can expand my spiritual self even further. I'm cutting those cords that held me back. I continue to work at healing my heart, and my love for myself gets stronger. I realized I didn't even know who I was until recently, so I'm excited about this part of my journey.

I now have my little crystal shop and love her so much. Now and again, the worry about money creeps in, but I try not to give those thoughts any momentum. I trust in my universe to provide, and I get by. New opportunities arrive without prior warning, and it's so exciting. The most important thing is that I am happy in my own world, which is expanding daily. Here I am writing in a book that you are reading. I never *ever* thought I'd be telling you my story. I'm so very proud of myself. Someone I know said to me that I sell energy. I'd not thought of it that way, but crystals are energy created by Mother Earth. Isn't that amazing?

The thing I've learned is that the universe always has your back. What we create or react to in our lives will affect the outcome. You can block a goal by constantly trying too hard.

Jenny Arnold

Just plant the seed, wait for it to flourish, and learn how to manifest. Listening to Esther Hicks helped me refocus my thoughts and behaviors to be in the receiving mode for my manifestations. I'd just put her on while in the car wherever I drove. It certainly worked for me as once I was in receiving mode, within a week, I was offered two shops for rent, a clinic to practice in, and three offers for rooms to teach reiki.

I've embraced negative contrast occurring and not analyzed the reasoning and found I'm given clear messages to conquer the issue, or I've seen the lesson behind it. Other people's behavior is not under your control, but how you let it control your reaction is. I think that's the hardest thing I've had to learn, especially after years of emotional programming and constant fight-or-flight nervous tension for as long as I can remember. It's time to be free.

I've noticed a clear divide between the spiritually awake and the *fast asleep*. It makes me quite sad to see and feel the fear people hold onto these days since the world changed in 2020 with COVID-19. However, positivity is now starting to overcome negativity, and the healing vibrations of the world are rising. Once you wake up, everything becomes so clear. I feel that this is my soul's purpose—to help raise earth's vibrations and help guide those who need to find their own connections and journeys.

My advice to anyone starting their own journey is to practice meditation daily, which helps bring so much clarity—keeping your chakras balanced, healing past traumas, cutting those cords from the past, healing ancestral wounds, carrying crystals, and eating clean as much as possible. Don't forget to treat yourself, too, though. Healing the soul and feeling your own power is essential, don't be afraid of losing that friendship, family member, or significant relationship. If these connections are meant to remain, they will be supportive. You will be guided elsewhere if they are no longer needed in your life. Finally, don't be afraid to take that leap of faith and see where it takes you. The universe has your back, and I know which way I'm going.

About Jenny

I moved from the UK to Western Australia in 2013 with my children and made a home in the Northern Suburbs of Perth. I qualified as a holistic therapist and reiki master in 2000 and wanted to incorporate these skills into helping women. I gained a Bachelor of Midwifery from the University of Nottingham in 2007. I became a lactation consultant in 2019. I had a passion for empowering women postnatally, with their breastfeeding journeys and improving their mental health.

Following a breast cancer diagnosis in 2018, major operations, and recovery, I focused my life on better health and sought more solutions to change the world around me. I started on my own self-empowerment and started to embrace my own spiritual journey. I, unfortunately, lost my employment as a midwife due to COVID-19 vaccine mandates in

Jenny Arnold

2021, choosing not to due to my own health concerns. I had to view life differently and create new visions.

The universe guided me to my ultimate dream job. I opened a small crystal shop at Hillarys Boat Harbour, Perth, and I can also be found at markets held in and around Perth. I hold regular reiki workshops in order to support women in their healing and spiritual journeys. I continue to grow within myself and develop an amazing network of friends and collaborations in the healing modalities.

Find me at:
Facebook: facebook.com/motherearthscrystals
Instagram: instagram.com/motherearthscrystals21
Email: motherearthscrystals@hotmail.com

Conny Wladkowski

SPIRITUAL AWAKENING

When I started writing this chapter, I spent quite a bit of time looking at the terminology *spiritual awakening* and asking myself what spiritual awakening is.

You can define spiritual awakening in so many different ways. It's a phrase that has become more and more in fashion. There is really no one set definition for it, no right or wrong. More and more people are opening up about their awakening. I find it is such a personal experience that there are many different ways to explain it because it differs for everyone.

So, before I keep writing about my own awakening, let me define what it means to me.

To be spiritually awakened means you are in a place of inner knowing and of trusting your *own* intuition. It means you know what is going on with you and your body and what is right and best for you. You don't need answers from anyone. Whatever someone says to you, it doesn't rock your inner world and beliefs. You know your own worth and what you stand for you. You do all this with ease and grace, accepting everyone for where they are on their own journey.

Many people experience spiritual awakening because of a life-altering, mind-blowing event, and everything suddenly changes for them. My spiritual awakening came from a combination of big events, learnings, and shifts over the years. I was more of a slow burner. I didn't have that one mind-blowing event that suddenly, from one day to another, changed everything, changed my awareness. For me, it was more of a steady process over the years.

I think that is the beauty of awakening. It happens differently for everyone, but however it happens for you *is* perfect for you. Not everyone needs to have a near-death experience to have an awakening. For some, like me, it has been a slower and longer journey of growth and learning. Ralph Waldo Emmerson said, 'It's not the destination, it's the journey.' And this has been true for me, although I can normally be quite impatient. To be honest, when I used to hear people say that, it triggered me so bad I couldn't stand it.

However, in the past few years, I have learned to embrace this journey of learning to trust myself, trust my intuition, and believe in myself. Don't get me wrong, this journey hasn't always been fun and easy, but it is all worth it. I had to overcome many challenges like everyone in life, some of which I didn't think I would be able to deal with. Sometimes I felt like the universe was throwing them at me left, right, and center.

Of course, challenges still come my way. This year has probably been one of the hardest, but I embrace challenges now rather than fear them. I know that every challenge is an opportunity. Before my awakening, I would've been upset and would always ask myself, *Why me? Why do I get all those challenges thrown at me?* I often felt defeated, like I didn't have much luck, and I felt angry. I just looked at the bad side of the challenge and situation and didn't see the growth, learning, and opportunity that came out of it.

Now I handle it totally differently. Don't get me wrong, sometimes I have the initial anger and frustration, but that usually doesn't last very long. Then I'm ready to deal with it and look at the positives, learning, and growth.

Life will always throw challenges at us. We can't avoid that. However, we can control how we deal with it and if we grow from it. It is one hundred percent our responsibility what we make out of it and what we learn from it. It sometimes sucks when we go through a tough time, but it is so amazing and freeing when we come out of it feeling on top.

I had my first glimpses of awakening at a very young age. I have always had this dream to make the world a better place. At fifteen, I discovered reiki and energy work. I realized there is more out there than we see and are told. Learning reiki was a big eye-opening experience for me, to just understand and see and realize that there is more than the life most of us are living.

I don't think I completely understood back then what *more* meant, but it definitely opened my senses and interest to discover what it was. As I was going through my teenage years, I felt torn between what *normal* teenagers did and discovering more about spirituality and other realms. I didn't find anyone my age who shared that interest with me. So, I hung out with friends my age on some weekends, and some weekends I spent with my reiki teacher or attending workshops about energy, self-growth, and angels. I always remember being the youngest at those workshops and often felt a little out of place. However, I often felt out of place hanging out with friends my age too. It felt like I didn't belong anywhere.

My spiritual awakening accelerated when I took responsibility for my *own* healing and stopped blaming the past for my actions, reactions, and future. When I finally decided to look at my trauma, and when I say look, I mean *really* look at it, feel it and heal from it, I stopped convincing myself that my life was perfect and that what happened in the past hadn't affected me just because I was too scared to look at it.

This all started with my dad's passing. He suddenly and unexpectedly passed away a few years ago. I was extremely close with him. His death not only left a big void in my life but was probably one of the hardest challenges in my life. It also made me change my career and start this journey of deeply healing myself.

After months of being in a big, dark hole, I decided that the challenge of Dad's death had a deeper meaning. I wanted to make my dad proud, stop wasting time, and start living my life doing my calling and passion. I wanted to fulfill the deeper meaning of why I'm actually on this earth. My passion, purpose, and dream were always to help other people heal.

My dream, at fifteen, was to make the world a better place. That dream hadn't changed. It was always in the back of my mind. I just doubted myself, that it was a ridiculous dream, a naive one, and that I wasn't good enough. I always had this calling internally, but I was too scared and had way too many limiting beliefs that I could never do this work. This intense, life-changing experience made me question everything and made me question who I was and what I really wanted to do.

It forced me to make changes in my life. So, I decided to start healing myself and become a hypnotherapist. I attended many different courses and immersive weekends that I used to learn how to help clients in the future and also to heal myself and overcome my own personal trauma. I always pushed myself out of my comfort zone and volunteered for any process because I knew it would help me heal myself.

I knew I needed to heal myself first to help others heal. As much as it scared me, having to look at my own trauma, I was done with all the excuses and finally started taking responsibility for my own healing and future. Healing myself and taking responsibility played a huge part in my own journey of awakening. As hard and as challenging as it often felt, in the end, it was one of the most rewarding experiences I had.

Conscious Revolution

Out of this experience, I became a hypnotherapist specializing in childhood trauma, and I have created my own process to help people heal from their trauma. A big part of the process I've created comes from my healing journey, inner knowing, and intuition. This is why I can now work with my clients individually, in a very client-approached way, because I can tune into what they need. I have that inner feeling, that inner knowing of how I can best help them heal themselves. I find this so important because every single person is different and has their own journey, so the approach I take suits exactly that person's needs. Too often, people are labeled, and the approach to help them depends on their label. Humans are not machines that can all be labeled and put in boxes.

Everything changed for me when I started healing from my own trauma and past. I was suddenly able to recognize my *own* worth. I used to be shy and uncomfortable, too scared to stand out. I always blended in and never wanted to be the center of attention. I lacked confidence and had no idea who I was.

When I started healing, I gained confidence and self-worth. I learned how to love myself unconditionally and found myself. I stopped comparing myself to others and judging myself and others. I started living my purpose and passion, helping people heal and improving this world. Being able to serve my clients and help them heal and overcome their blockages is the most heart-filling and rewarding experience in my life.

This is why I'm on earth. *This* is the purpose I live for every single day. It is simply beautiful to connect with my clients on such a deep level, where deep healing takes place. When it comes to healing from trauma, connection and trust are so important. That deep connection was only possible once I let go of my ego and judgment.

I have also made *so* many beautiful connections with like-minded people I met at workshops and courses. This has helped me to further my own awakening and get through the rough patches and challenging times.

I finally found my tribe of people, and suddenly I didn't feel out of place anymore like how I felt growing up as a teenager.

I started to feel like I had people around me who understood me, often sharing the same purpose to help people heal. This is also the tribe of people that, even today, I reach out to when I'm struggling or need help. Asking for help was something I never used to be good at. Before my awakening, asking for help meant weakness and triggered that limiting belief that I wasn't good enough. So, I went through life burned out and tired and felt like I had to do everything alone. I preferred that to being judged by people around me or even judging myself for it.

I have totally turned that around and changed my view, and I believe wholeheartedly that nobody should go through life alone and that asking for help shows strength. We all need a village around us and support and help each other free of judgment. When the right people surround you, there is no judgment, there is love and support, and they absolutely want to help you.

Since my awakening, my intuition and inner knowing have been loud and clear. I can tune into my own body and know what is going on inside of me. I hardly ever look for outside answers or reassurance anymore. I know what my body and mind need and can tune into what messages my body sends me. I know what and who feels good for me, and I have developed a strong connection with my own spirit guides. I'm convinced that we all have spirit guides from the moment we're born. We have our own unique guides that are here to support us, protect us, and care for us. We just have to believe in them, that they are here, and ask them for help.

I often ask mine for help, and the more I started communicating with them, the more they showed up for me. Don't get me wrong, in the beginning, I was very skeptical about having spirit guides, but once I opened myself up to the possibility, I started experiencing them. The more I opened up and communicated with them, my belief and connection grew stronger. Some people see them, some feel them or hear their spirit guides. For me, it is an inner knowing, almost like a voice within myself. Again, there is no wrong or right. It is all about how *you* experience them. I encourage you to start connecting with your guides. The more you ask for help, the more you receive. You could also ask them for signs showing you they are present. Allow yourself to open up to their guidance and messages. This can take a bit of practice, but it is also a lot of fun. As challenging as spiritual awakening is, let's not forget to incorporate some fun into it.

If you are going through your own awakening, I encourage you to keep going. As tough and confusing as it often might feel, it's all worth it in the end. You may lose people on the way who are stuck in their model of the world and can't understand why you are changing. That can sometimes feel painful, but you will gain new connections with like-minded people. Alexander Graham Bell once said, 'When one door closes, another door opens.' Those connections will be more authentic and deeper than you can ever imagine.

Spiritual awakening is often very confusing at first. You might be questioning everything you ever thought was true. Who are you? Why are you on earth? What is your purpose? Step out of your comfort zone and jump into the unknown and into your growth zone. Oh yes, that is quite scary and challenging, but this is where you grow, you get rewarded, and change happens.

It's such an exciting zone to be in. And after a little while, your growth becomes your new comfort zone. Then you can step out of that again into your new growth zone. Once you start this, it almost becomes like an addiction, but a good one. It feels uncomfortable at first, but then it will feel great and rewarding, and so many new opportunities will open up for you.

Maybe you already know what you want to do and how you want to change your life because you have a lifelong calling. Or maybe you just know your old comfort zone is not working for you anymore, and you just need to try out different things and see what feels right and good for you, which is fun and exciting.

I was stuck in my comfort zone for a long time. I was working a job that didn't fulfill me, living with habits that didn't serve me, and hanging around people that were negative and clearly weren't good for me. But once I stepped out of my comfort zone into my new growth zone, followed my dream and passion, stepped into my true self, and started helping people, I started feeling complete and feeling joy in my life. As scary as it was to give up my full-time job, look at my own trauma, and change my career, it was the most rewarding thing I have ever done.

One of the most important habits I've incorporated daily is to stop and reflect. I often reflect on my emotions and behaviors to understand why I react and feel certain ways. I do this with love and kindness to find out what is going on in the layers of my subconscious mind and to see how I can grow. I have definitely learned to be kinder to myself, and rather than those emotions affecting me, I now study and learn from them. While I still like to grow, I do accept myself with all my imperfections and flaws. This has helped me to become a lot more peaceful and calm.

I still practice all these things daily and sometimes catch myself falling back into old habits. Into what we have been preached and conditioned to do from birth. Where I catch myself and let other people's words affect me and question my own beliefs and my own inner knowing. I know this will be a lifelong practice, kind of like a lifelong journey with no end destination, but I know I'm getting better and better at it every day. Every day I feel freer and happier knowing that everything I need is within. Every answer I need, I already have.

About Conny

Hello, I'm Conny Wladkowski.

I'm a hypnotherapist, self-healing coach, author, and international presenter.

I'm the creator of the SHINE your inner child process and the Break Free from Anxiety EASIER process.

Originally born in Austria, I was on the path of wanting to heal myself and others from a very young age. I was only fifteen when I first studied energy healing, which was my introduction to the world of self-healing and self-empowerment.

After experiencing serious health issues at the age of twenty-five, I knew I had to make major changes to live a happy and healthy life!

Physically, I recovered, but emotionally, I struggled to recover from my health issues. I lived with severe panic attacks for several years and struggled to cope with life. Life was a constant struggle, and I was just surviving.

Then out of the blue, my dad, whom I was very close to, suddenly passed away, which made me spiral into a big, black hole.

This was one of the biggest challenges in my life, but also a very important point in my conscious awakening. This was the moment I decided to stop wasting my time and live my true purpose.

I learned everything about hypnotherapy, completely got rid of my panic attacks, and started living again. This was such a profound experience for me that I decided to change my career and learn the most amazing and powerful tools. Feeling so free after having lived in so much fear and panic for such a long time has led to my passion for helping other people!

Having learned multiple modalities for over twenty years, combined with my own life experiences and healing journey, I have created some magical and profound processes.

I specialize in anxiety and childhood trauma relief.

I provide a safe space, free of judgment, full of love and holding. This then allows healing to take place so that my clients can be the best version of themselves and thrive in life.

Find me at:
Website: besthypnotherapymelbourne.com.au
YouTube: youtube.com/channel/UClSFh4baymeMVpSU-n8Eaow
Instagram: instagram.com/right_time_to_shine
Facebook: facebook.com/connywladkowski

Jade Bell

A WAY FORWARD

When the idea for this book came across my desk, I told a friend I couldn't write for it because I'd never had a conscious revolution. She answered with, 'What? Yes, you have.'

It got me thinking, what is a conscious revolution? What does it mean to me? And if I define it, have I had any?

Well, yes, many. I'm an ever-evolving being. While thinking about the brief, I realized that a conscious revolution could be an individualized ideology. Of course, there is a definition, albeit marginally ambiguous. How it applies to you may differ from how it applies to me. It's a mutually exclusive evolution if we talk about individuals and not as it pertains to the societal notions of a conscious collective for change. It may be small, or it may be big, but it's relative.

Considering the idea of a conscious revolution individualized to me got me thinking about how many I've had. How far back did they go?

What is the trajectory of evolution for me? And are there grey areas to the word conscious? For instance, can a child have a conscious revolution in response to a traumatic event but not understand that they've had one? Would it be conscious or unconscious?

I wondered if the memory of the silhouetted woman in the doorway, slowly dissipating until it was gone, was the moment that little me made a decision that impacted my life until two years ago. I stood at the bottom of our tiled staircase, looking at the door, a chill cradling my bare feet. The sun was at her back, and I felt so small. In the memory that belongs to a child, she was colossal until she drifted and became smaller and smaller. This memory symbolizes a pivotal moment for me going forward in my life. In retrospect, it was the catalyst for holding onto people, even when I shouldn't. Was this a conscious revolution? To hold on too tight because of the fear of losing people?

Take this definition from the American Psychological Association (n.d.), 'Experiential or subjective interpretations, however, define consciousness in terms of mental imagery; intuition; subjective experience as related to sensations, perceptions, emotions, moods, and dreams; self-awareness; awareness of awareness itself and of the unity between the self and others and the physical world; stream of consciousness; and other aspects of private experience.'

I could argue that, yes, this moment was a conscious revolution. The idea that the sensation and emotion of my one constant until I was five leaving caused a ripple effect that took a pandemic for me to acknowledge was a problem and finally to alter. But once I chose to be okay with filtering what I allowed in, I felt free. But that undoing of forty-one years of conditioning was harrowing.

Since COVID-19, I have found myself being more insular. The once almost addictive need to be social waned rapidly and left me in freefall, wondering who the hell I was when I wasn't surrounded by people. I couldn't contend with the noise on the outside and how it affected the noise that deafened me on the inside. All the noise was overwhelming, and I crumbled under the weight.

I stopped looking out at the world and started looking as far as my three children, my marriage, and myself.

I realized I spent years being there for everyone else and neglected myself. I eradicated toxic relationships from my life and stopped allowing situations that didn't feel right in my being. All the extra people and things I thought I needed fell away. It wasn't anyone's fault that relationships were toxic. I'm not saying the people were toxic, and I'm not blaming others for the breakdown in relationships. I had zero ability to set boundaries because I was scared of losing people. But I realized that letting go of people is healthy and a critical growth phase. And the people who peeled off as a result also provided an invaluable lesson. One that gave me peace.

It was such a strange thing for me to let go of people. It was so hard because I'd never really said that's enough to anyone. I always thought I wasn't *me* without all the people, but I realized I wasn't me with them. I mourned the friendships that fell away, but by closing my life to many, I finally felt free.

The pandemic wasn't the catalyst for a conscious revolution, in retrospect, but it drove it harder and faster than if no pandemic existed.

If you consider moments where you've decided on a change and driven yourself forward to that purpose, you are consciously evolving. Acknowledging my conscious revolutions came in floods once I thought about times when I chose to change. One of the most important and positive needs for change came when I fell pregnant with our first child. This one moment began the evolution toward a better life. One where learning is paramount and constant reflection is integral.

I have lived two very separate lives in two very different worlds. So much so that when I had my first child and moved to a semirural community, I felt like I was in the twilight zone. I wasn't sure if this new world was real or a dream and I was somehow still tethered to the old, which

I realize now, through trauma, I was. For a long time, the threads from that other life pulled taunt, reminding me of things I'd rather forget, of moments that made me believe this new life wasn't anything I could possibly deserve. I went from dealing with the dark underbelly of society to baking cakes and going to mothers' groups. Everything changed for me.

Everything needed to change.

Don't get me wrong, it wasn't all bad. I met some wonderful people with whom I'm still friends, and I met my husband. But the bad far outweighed the good. That 'other' life wasn't conducive to children. It was barely conducive for an adult.

There were many years of abusive behavior from others, but I did much of it to me, driven by an utter lack of self-worth and guidance as a young woman. I balanced on a cliff of needing people to want me, love me, and not leave me. The endless weeks of bouncing from one party to the next while running a club driven by men and women who used young people and their brokenness to their advantage were systemically damaging. The drugs, near-death experiences, grooming, and the solid belief that offering my body made people love me drove me to places that took many years to undo. Even now, that trauma resides. The loss and the inexplicable darkness weren't a life. It was survival, but only just.

There isn't a moment when I think back on that young woman when she saw a clear future. If I hadn't fallen pregnant, I'm not sure what my world would look like now. If that world kept me, I'd be a shell of bitterness. It has a way of extracting your goodness and sucking out the light. However, I learned many valuable lessons, and there was a time when I felt that world gave me power as a woman. But in the end, it would have eroded me even more if I had stayed. The decay already made me unrecognizable to myself, not that I was certain I knew who I was before that time. What I did know was when I left that life, I didn't know how to live outside of an environment that shaped the person I'd become.

Conscious Revolution

I decided to let that world and all in it fall away. The journey out was easier because my best friend came with me, and we started building a life. He and my children saved my life. Actually, I saved my life because, ultimately, I chose to evolve, but they gave me the push. The overwhelming need to be better for them and to always learn and reflect pushed me onto a path that my seventeen-year-old—even my thirty-year-old—self never thought possible.

One change, one choice to be a different kind of human, was the boulder in the river. I know the analogy is a pebble in a pond, but I can assure you it felt like a boulder blocking a raging torrent at the time. But I wanted a calmer life, so it didn't matter that it was hard to find a person I liked when I looked in the mirror. That person had so much growth to do so she could move forward and be a mum, and I welcomed it. I had to do it because, under the waves of pain, I felt that anything was possible and that the world lay out in front of me, uncharted with infinite possibilities. I had a second chance, or was it a third? I won't split hairs. I had it, but what the fuck was I going to do with it?

Well, for starters, muddle through the first years of being a mum. We had trouble having kids. They never stuck. We were told the chances of us conceiving and a baby making it full-term were one in a million. If I get existential about this news and the ones we lost, I think those souls knew I wasn't ready to be a mum. But with my first child, I sat bolt upright in the early morning hours and took a pregnancy test. The two lines popped up like before, but the feeling was different. This soul wanted me, and I knew this baby would make it the entire way.

This baby was a fighter. At eight weeks gestation, I had surgery to remove my appendix. They told me in recovery that ninety-eight percent of babies don't make it because they can't do keyhole surgery. But she did. Her birth was traumatic for her. She wasn't breathing, and the panic in the room didn't register for me until days later because, in my mind, I knew she would be okay. Once she was awake, she was wideawake, and she absorbed the world magically. She still does. She sees things others don't. She functions on a different and glorious level.

She didn't, however, sleep. Like ever! Those were hard times. I came from a world where babies weren't a thing. I was never around them. So, when I had my own, I was isolated and alone with the challenges I faced. Breastfeeding wasn't like in the movies; women didn't just bounce back after birth. For one, no one told me about the mess pushing a human out would do to my vagina.

We did in-vitro fertilization (IVF) for our second child. That process was a series of painful operations and procedures, but it was worth every moment because she is a beautiful human, full of love and grace. Then I fell pregnant with our third two months after the second was born. She is a fierce little woman who will rule the world. Without IVF, I believe we wouldn't have had either of our last two babies. I also believe that our youngest chose her sister to be her soulmate as much as she chose me to be her mum.

In three years and nine months, I went from being a person who treated her body and her being like dirt to a mum of three little girls. Three babies. None of whom slept. My husband was fly-in fly-out, and family was scarce and mostly non-existent. Yep, full-blown twilight zone. Thankfully, I was surrounded by amazing girlfriends, all going through similar things. But regardless of how little sleep I managed or how discombobulated I felt daily, I had another conscious revolution.

I knew one day I wanted a career that had nothing to do with my previous skill set. Let's face it, that industry isn't great for families because it requires weekend work, and after leaving, it wasn't something I wanted to invite back. Another change was needed. I wanted a job I could work around my kids. I wanted to be available to them. While reflecting on these thoughts about being present for my kids, I was driven back to my childhood and again pondered what a conscious revolution meant.

This need to be there for my girls came from my sadness when parental presence wasn't available when I was younger. There is a part of me, and I'm not blaming anyone because my parents did their best, which acknowledges that the lack of enforced boundaries allowed me to wander off any decent path as a teenager. As I said, there is no blame in my pondering. Working was essential for my parents. There wasn't any room for a stay-at-home scenario. But it untethers a child when there isn't someone present when needed.

It's also important for me to acknowledge the limitations placed on my parents by their parents. There was generational hamstringing of their potential as people and parents. But this is how we generationally grow. We take from the ones before and learn to evolve beyond that, understanding what we want to impart. It was nobody's fault that my brother and I were free-range. It was born out of necessity and the need to provide. But looking back on my childhood, those moments when I longed for someone to be present sparked my need to be there for my kids. Thankfully, the life my partner and I created, and his career choice, facilitated this. The moments of sadness I felt as a child imprinted on me and led me to a conscious revolution, albeit unconsciously.

I wanted a job where I didn't have to give up dropping my kids at school and picking them up. I wanted a job where I could attend school exhibitions and be there when they received awards or cheer on the sidelines at sports carnivals. I wanted a job that I could mold my life around, not my life around my job. So I started studying. First at the Australian School of Journalism, then a Bachelor of Arts in Writing and Publishing that I'm still chipping away at.

Choosing to study was difficult with three little kids, but it opened a whole new world for me, a world I never thought I could navigate and be successful. It not only opened a career path that allowed me to be with my kids, but all the writing prompted me to delve into the 'other' world and start processing the past.

This is still a work in progress and will be for a long time. One thing that's helped me is finding martial arts. It will humble you, remove your ego, and make you question why you do what you do. It encourages you to evaluate yourself. I found a space in my life for something that is for me and allows me time to let the world fall away.

I had a discussion one afternoon with a friend about what constitutes a meditative state. She was reading a how-to meditation book and suggested that sitting quietly and clearing your mind was the only way. I don't believe this for myself. Being on the mats and doing jiujitsu is the only time I feel at peace, other than when I'm writing, but that's an entirely different thing for me. I don't think about anything outside that space. I'm connected completely and deeply to that moment.

Being comfortable in uncomfortable situations and having control has helped me heal past abuse-related trauma. I'm so grateful the universe led me to that safe place. But writing ultimately facilitated this stage of my conscious revolution. Writing your truth is powerful if you allow yourself to really indulge. It's terrifying, cathartic, overwhelming, and positively soul enriching, but it takes a level of brave to reach inside and be truthful, to write like you aren't writing for anyone but yourself. It's the ultimate experiment in vulnerability.

Allowing myself to feel free enough to let the words out changed my life. But it all began with a simple, well, kind of, choice to change, grow, and be better. Isn't allowing yourself the space to reflect the most beautiful thing? You can learn so much.

Choosing to change opened so many more doors. I was fearful through most of it but did it anyway. I find now that if I feel fear when making a change, I'm usually on the right track. For example, this year, I chose to put my studies aside and say yes to a job opportunity. I was terrified! But went in headfirst because, as my friend says, 'What's the worst that can happen?'

It's my dream job in the field I've wanted to be in since I was little. I get to do something I love with extraordinary people.

Conscious Revolution

Now that I'm at the end of this piece, I think, for me, conscious revolution is a constant evolution. I hope never to stop growing, learning, and evolving because it's beautiful, and when I get to the end of it all, I will safely say, 'Man, I lived, loved, and learned.'

About Jade

Hi, I'm Jade, author and chief editor for Maven Press. I live in the beautiful Perth Hills with my three daughters, husband, dogs, and chickens. I feel like I'm a perpetual scholar, always seeking to learn something.

My days are spent raising my girls, who force me to question myself in the hope I can always do better for them and learn from past trauma. A fair portion of my time is given to challenging not only my physical self but also my spiritual self in martial arts. Reading and writing keep the creativity flowing.

I believe in giving a platform to people with a story. If one sentence in this book resonates with someone, then we have done something.

It's been a privilege to edit and read these chapters from amazing, brave women willing to tell their stories. I'm grateful for my journey and the distance I've traveled from my beginning to now.

Laura Elizabeth

THE CHOICE IS YOURS

Since receiving the inspiration for this anthology, my perception and understanding of a conscious revolution have changed significantly. It is no surprise, as nothing I do is without the intention of personal growth for all involved in the books we birth. For me, I always intended the process of writing to be a journey of deep catharsis and transformation. However, with a title like *Conscious Revolution*, I understand now that writing for this book was like a cry for help from the lost little fragments of my soul. The power of this process has left no stone unturned and given me a series of unforgettable ah ha! moments.

Identity has been something I have struggled with my entire life. Never really knowing where I belonged or how I was supposed to fit in. Mimicking the talents and traits of others I admired around me, who seemed so confident and effortless in being themselves, is what got me through my awkward teens. Eventually, somewhere in my late teens, I adopted the belief that spirituality was my 'thing'. I always had a keen sense of intuition and sat comfortably in this space, so it felt like the most appropriate label to adopt. Everyone around me was accepting, and I became known as the 'spiritual' one, the airy-fairy one, the psychic one. It just made sense.

In recent months, I have come to understand that this was just another distraction from the truth of who I am. I am highly skilled with my energy and bodywork because I stay in my lane and focus on the pain and challenges I know in my core. Clients travel vast distances to work with me to heal shame and trauma. Specifically, I work with clients who store shame and trauma around sexual abuse, birth trauma, body image, mother line trauma, intimacy and relationships, eating disorders, mother guilt, anxiety, cycles of over-giving, and burnout, to name a few. These are issues I have lived experience with and overcome, often more than once in this lifetime. To these clients, I have changed their lives. I have asked the right questions. I have let them cry, and I have allowed them to feel heard. Nothing they can says or do within this context will ever shock me or create judgment. My work, my purpose, is my superpower, and I can easily transfer it from one modality to the next.

But the deeper I dove my own consciousness into the realms of spirituality, the more comfortable it felt to hide in the ether and the more I could bypass the grittiness and shame of life and focus on helping others. I must sit with the guilt and shame of this realization before I came to write about it. How could I possibly help others when there are parts within me unhealed and more layers to uncover? Will everyone think I am a fraud? Is my work and my service enough?

But we don't know what we don't know, and the difference is in the awareness. When we know better, then we have a responsibility to do better. So, this is a declaration and an apology to anyone who has felt betrayed as I launched myself into creating experiences for them to heal and transform while I was still in various seasons of my own life and learning. I must trust that those drawn into my services are there for a reason and will receive exactly what they need. And so it is.

Earlier this year, I found myself deep in one of those healing cycles. I was anxious to the point of self-harm. I wasn't eating, and I was enmeshed in an emotionally abusive relationship that I was trying to fool myself wasn't. I ran workshops on empowerment and manifesting to create your dream life, but I was harboring and so articulately perpetuating the belief that I am not enough. I felt broken. My body was inflamed, and I became more and more unwell.

One day, feeling completely hopeless, I sat in contemplation with plant medicine. The journey began slowly and gently, and it felt safe to surrender. Then, at the peak of this medicine journey, clear as day, the words 'you are enough now' came through on what felt like a loudspeaker as I sobbed in the bathroom. It lit up every cell of my being. It felt like the pain of lifetimes came together at zero point, and suddenly, it clicked … I am enough.

Everything in my life (and lifetimes past) is a choice. I magnetized everything in my life based on the belief that I was not enough. I choose to stay stuck here or choose to illuminate the bliss and success that comes with the truth of *enoughness*. Since that moment, that conversation with myself, I have consciously chosen life from a space of being enough. And EVERYTHING has changed. Everything! The moment I accepted that life happens *for* me and not *to* me was the moment I took radical self-responsibility for my thoughts, my actions, and my life.

Understanding this, along with letting go of any need for life to fit into preconceived ideas or look a certain way, was like uncovering a glitch in the matrix. It felt like the path to freedom. It felt like, after years of existing, I finally came to know my purpose. I AM ENOUGH.

I don't need trinkets, crystals, deities, or rituals to prove it. I simply just choose in every conscious moment to believe it. I no longer need to manifest success and joy and a life filled with love, looking outside this truth, because I am it. In every waking moment, I choose it, and therefore it is.

I wish I had a formula or a workbook to show you the process. To give you something tangible that helps it all click into place, but it would surely complicate and dramatize the simplicity of the truth.

As human beings, we tend to overthink, overanalyze, and complicate our lives. Often the answers we need and the truth we seek are as simple as a few big, deep breaths and taking it right back to simple. Any time I have swayed from my path this year, I take a breath and repeat 'I am enough' until it feels like home again. Until my nervous system relaxes and the emergency is over, and everything is and always will be fine because 'I am enough'.

I'm not sure what this change in me holds for the future of my service. As I continue to grow, learn, and evolve, I know there is an evolution in the process. I am humbled by the clients who have trusted me with their lives, and I am excited to call in the new humans magnetized to what comes next.

One thing I know for certain is that there is only change, and with each change, we have choices. The more we execute our choices from a place of simple objectivity, the clearer the path ahead. That's not to say we shouldn't celebrate our wins and grieve our losses. As human beings, we are intrinsically wired to our emotional programming, but imagine if you had the conscious awareness and the knowing when to surrender to the feels. Would life look different for you? Would you feel clearer? Would you be more open to taking risks and walking into new opportunities, knowing that life is happening for you at every moment?

I'm so humbled that you chose to pick up this book and soak in the words of these divine women. I can't tell you what will happen next, but I know that if just one word from one chapter has ignited something within you, we have collectively served our purpose in this conscious revolution.

About Laura

Hi, I'm Laura Elizabeth, a trailblazing changemaker and advocate for women's empowerment, author of nine bestselling titles, director at Maven Press, *creatress* of Kuntea, and owner of Laura Elizabeth Wellness.

I am dedicated to creating intimate experiences for conscious women ready to step into a deeper layer of understanding of themselves. I assist them in embracing and embodying their sensuality, reclaiming their voices, and owning their personal power.

I offer womb and yoni massage therapy, reiki attunements, and a catalogue of workshops, education and training events online and in person with a focus on women's health.

I am also the woman behind a steadfast, hand-crafted organic product range topping its tenth year, including the risqué yoni steaming brand Kuntea for reproductive health and wellness.

Laura Elizabeth

My love of writing and being a keeper of women's stories has led me most recently to create Maven Press Publishing. I am delighted to doula storytellers through the conception, gestation, and birth of their books into the world as they step deeper into their truth as changemakers.

A naturally gifted psychic medium born on the East Coast of Fife, Scotland, I immigrated to Perth, Western Australia, as a pre-teen in 1999. With two decades of experience cultivating my skills as an energy worker and holding space for clients, I offer the safest and most profoundly intimate containers for women to encounter deep transformation.

A boundary pusher and taboo smasher, I am best known for my real, quirky, and honest guidance, ensuring the deepest empathy and understanding without judgment. I believe keeping a healthy sense of humor is important to stay grounded and authentic.

My service to clients is most definitely a niche. Yet, I believe it is the real missing link in human connection and healing for women. We are programmed to think, feel, and do based on the needs of others. But we unleash our real magic when we set aside time to explore honoring, nurturing, and loving ourselves back into a belief of radical acceptance and remembering our magnificence.

A passionate solo mother of three, leading by example, smashing goals, and living with purpose, I hope to be a positive influence and for my own children to reach their full potential and inspire others to do the same.

I hold your hand and love you while you remember how to love yourself.

Website: lauraelizabeth.com.au
Facebook: facebook.com/eroticmavenmedicine
Instagram: instagram.com/eroticmaven_medicine
Instagram: instagram.com/kuntea_by_le
Website: mavenpress.com.au
Instagram: instagram.com/mavenpress

References

mavenpress.com.au/cr-references

www.ingramcontent.com/pod-product-compliance
Lightning Source LLC
Chambersburg PA
CBHW020324010526
44107CB00054B/1964